This revised Code of Practice deals with the duties placed by Part III of the Disability Discrimination Act 1995 on those providing goods, facilities or services to the public and those selling, letting or managing premises. The Act makes it unlawful for service providers, landlords and other persons to discriminate against disabled people in certain circumstances.

The duties on service providers are being introduced in three stages:

- since 2 December 1996, it has been unlawful for service providers to treat disabled people less favourably for a reason related to their disability;

- from 1 October 1999, service providers have to make "reasonable adjustments" for disabled people, such as providing extra help or making changes to the way they provide their services; and

- it is intended that, from 2004, service providers will also have to make "reasonable adjustments" to the physical features of their premises to overcome physical barriers to access.

The duties on landlords and other persons in connection with the selling, letting and managing of premises were introduced on 2 December 1996. Since that date it has been unlawful for them to treat disabled people less favourably for a reason related to their disability. There is no equivalent duty to make "reasonable adjustments" in relation to those premises.

The original Code, which was issued in July 1996, has been revised in the light of experience gained since the first duties were implemented in December 1996 and to take account of the new duties on service providers. This Code replaces the original Code.

Chapter 10 of the Code sets out ways in which service providers, landlords and other persons can avoid acting unlawfully and enable disabled people to participate fully in society.

Contents

1 **Introduction** 4
Purpose of Part III of the Act 4
Purpose of the Code 4
Status of the Code 4
How to use the Code 5
Examples in the Code 5
References in the Code 6
Further information 6

2 **What does the Act say about providing services?** 7
Introduction 7
What does the Act make unlawful? 7
What does the Act mean by "discrimination"? 7
Who has rights under the Act? 8
What services are affected by Part III of the Act? 9
What services are not affected? 11
Services not available to the public 13

3 **The service provider's duty not to treat a disabled person less favourably** 16
Introduction 16
What is unlawful? 16
Less favourable treatment 16
When is "less favourable treatment" unlawful discrimination? 17
Refusal or non-provision of service 19
Standard or manner of service 20
Terms of service 21
Can service providers treat a disabled person more favourably? 22

4 **Making changes for disabled people: the service provider's duty to make reasonable adjustments** 23
Introduction 23
What does the Act say? 23
What is the duty to make reasonable adjustments? 23
To whom is the duty to make reasonable adjustments owed? 24
At what point does the duty to make reasonable adjustments arise? 24
How long does the duty continue? 25
What is meant by "reasonable steps"? 25
What is "unreasonably difficult"? 28
What happens if the duty to make reasonable adjustments is not complied with? .. 28

5 **Reasonable adjustments in practice** 29
Introduction 29
Practices, policies and procedures 29
Reasonable adjustments and the physical features of premises 32
Auxiliary aids and services 35

£12.95

6 **Can a service provider justify less favourable treatment or failure to make reasonable adjustments?** 46
Introduction 46
Less favourable treatment 46
Failure to make reasonable adjustments 46
The general approach to justification 47
Health or safety 48
Incapacity to contract 49
Service provider otherwise unable to provide the service to the public 51
To enable the service provider to provide the service 52
Greater expense 53
Additional cost of providing the service 53
Protecting the fundamental nature of a business or service 54

7 **Special rules affecting insurance, guarantees and deposits** 56
Introduction 56
Insurance 56
Guarantees 59
Deposits 61

8 **Selling, letting or managing premises** 64
Introduction 64
What does the Act make unlawful? 64
What does the Act mean by "discrimination"? 65
Is there a duty to make adjustments in relation to premises? 66
What is a "disposal" under the Act? 66
What is meant by "premises" and "tenancy"? 66
Does the Act apply to all disposals of premises? 67
Disposal of premises 67
Management of premises 71
Licence or consent 73
Justifying less favourable treatment in relation to premises 73
Deposits 76

9 **Other provisions under the Act** 79
Introduction 79
Victimisation 79
Aiding unlawful acts 80
Liability for employees' and agents' acts 81
Terms of agreements 82
Statutory authority and national security 83
What happens if there is a dispute under the Act? 83
What happens if a dispute cannot be resolved? 84
Disability Rights Commission 84

10 **General guidance on good practice** 85
Introduction 85
Good practice and reasonable adjustments 86

Appendix: The meaning of disability 92

Index 96

1
2
3
4
5
6
7
8
9
10

1 Introduction

Purpose of Part III of the Act

1.1 On 2 December 1996, the Disability Discrimination Act 1995 (the Act) brought in measures to prevent discrimination against disabled people. Part III of the Act is based on the principle that disabled people should not be discriminated against by service providers or those involved in the disposal or management of premises. Subject to limited exceptions, anyone who comes within either of these categories must comply with the duties set out in Part III. It should be noted that those selling, letting or managing premises could also have duties as service providers.

Purpose of the Code

1.2 This Code of Practice (the Code) gives practical guidance on how to prevent discrimination against disabled people in accessing services or premises. It describes the duties on those providing services to the public and those selling, letting or managing premises under Part III of the Act. The Code helps disabled people to understand the law and assists service providers, landlords and other persons to avoid complaints and litigation by adopting good practice. It also aims to advance the elimination of discrimination against disabled people and to encourage good practice.

ss 51–54

1.3 The Secretary of State has issued this Code under the Act on the basis of proposals prepared by the National Disability Council. It applies to England, Wales and Scotland and comes into effect on 1 October 1999, replacing the original Code which was issued in 1996. A similar but separate Code applies to Northern Ireland.

Status of the Code

s 51(3)–(5)

1.4 The Code does not impose legal obligations. Nor is it an authoritative statement of the law – that is a matter for the courts. However, the Code can be used in evidence in legal proceedings under the Act. Courts (and, in respect of insurance services provided to employees, employment tribunals) must take into account any part of the Code that

4

appears to them relevant to any question arising in those proceedings. If service providers and those involved in selling, letting or managing premises follow the guidance in the Code, it may help to avoid an adverse judgment by a court in any proceedings.

How to use the Code

1.5 **This chapter** gives a general introduction to the Code and to Part III of the Act. **Chapters 2 – 7** deal with the duties on service providers, including a description of the duty to make reasonable adjustments for disabled people. **Chapter 8** deals with the duties on those selling, letting or managing premises. **Chapter 9** describes other actions made unlawful by the Act and explains what happens if discrimination is alleged. **Chapter 10** gives general guidance on avoiding discrimination and promoting good practice.

1.6 **The Appendix** gives more information on what is meant by disability and who are disabled persons. Separate statutory guidance relating to the definition of disability has been issued under the Act.

1.7 Each chapter of the Code should be viewed as part of an overall explanation of Part III of the Act and the regulations made under it. In order to understand the law properly it is necessary to read the Code as a whole. The Code should not be read too narrowly or literally. It is intended to explain the principles of the law, to illustrate how the Act might operate in certain situations and to provide general guidance on good practice. There are some questions which the Code cannot resolve and which must await the authoritative interpretation of the courts. The Code is not intended to be a substitute for taking appropriate advice on the legal consequences of particular situations.

Examples in the Code

1.8 Examples of good practice and how the Act is likely to work are given in boxes. They are intended simply to illustrate the principles and concepts used in the legislation and should be read in that light. The examples should not be treated as complete or authoritative statements of the law.

1.9   While the examples refer to particular situations, they should be understood more widely as demonstrating how the law is likely to be applied generally. They can often be used to test how the law might apply in analogous situations involving different disabilities, services or service providers. They attempt to use as many different varieties of disabilities and services as possible to demonstrate the width and scope of the Act. References to male or female disabled people are given for realism and could, of course, apply to either sex.

References in the Code

1.10   Throughout the Code, references are made to "service providers" for convenience. Subject to certain exceptions, Part III of the Act applies to any person or any organisation or entity which is concerned with the provision in the United Kingdom of services (including goods and facilities) to the public or a section of the public. Similarly, the Act applies to disabled people who use, or seek to use, the services so provided, whether as customers, buyers, shoppers, consumers, clients, patrons or service users.

1.11   References to the Act are shown in the margins. For example, s 1(1) means section 1(1) of the Act and Sch 1 means Schedule 1 to the Act. Where reference is made to regulations made under the Act, the Statutory Instrument number is shown in the margin (for example, SI 1996/1836).

Further information

1.12   Copies of the Act and regulations made under it (and further copies of this Code) can be purchased from the Stationery Office bookshops. A separate Code covering the employment provisions of the Act and guidance relating to the definition of disability are also available from the same source, as is a Code dealing with the duties of trade organisations to their disabled members and applicants.

1.13   Free information about the Act can be obtained by contacting the DDA Helpline:

Telephone: 0345 622 633
Faxback service: 0345 622 611
Textphone: 0345 622 644

The Code and information about the Act are also available in alternative formats or via the Internet [http://www.dfee.gov.uk].

What does the Act say about providing services?

Introduction

2.1 This chapter provides an overview of the provisions of Part III relating to the provision of services. It outlines what is made unlawful by the Act and explains what is meant by "discrimination". It describes the scope of services affected by the Act (and those which are excluded) and those people who have rights under the Act.

What does the Act make unlawful?

2.2 The Act makes it unlawful for a service provider to **discriminate** against a disabled person:

- by refusing to provide (or deliberately not providing) any service which it provides (or is prepared to provide) to members of the public; or

  s 19(1)(a)

- in the standard of service which it provides to the disabled person or the manner in which it provides it; or

  s 19(1)(c)

- in the terms on which it provides a service to the disabled person.

  s 19(1)(d)

References to providing a service include providing goods or facilities.

2.3 It is also unlawful for a service provider to **discriminate** in:

  s 19(1)(b)

- failing to comply with any duty imposed on it by section 21 (a duty to make reasonable adjustments) in circumstances in which the effect of that failure is to make it impossible or unreasonably difficult for the disabled person to make use of any such service.

The reference to making use of a service includes using goods or facilities.

What does the Act mean by "discrimination"?

2.4 The Act says that discrimination against a disabled person occurs in two possible ways.

s 20(1)

2.5 One way in which discrimination occurs is when a service provider:

- **treats the disabled person less favourably** – for a reason relating to the disabled person's disability – than it treats (or would treat) others to whom that reason does not (or would not) apply; **and**

- cannot show that the treatment is **justified**.

2.6 Making sure that a service provider does not treat a disabled person less favourably is considered in more detail in **Chapter 3** below. Whether and when a service provider might be able to justify the less favourable treatment of a disabled person is considered in **Chapter 6** below.

s 20(2)

2.7 The other way in which discrimination occurs is when a service provider:

- fails to comply with a duty imposed on it by section 21 of the Act (a duty to make **"reasonable adjustments"**) in relation to the disabled person; **and**

- cannot show that the failure is **justified**.

2.8 The duty to make reasonable adjustments is covered in greater detail in **Chapters 4 and 5** below. Whether and when a service provider might be able to justify a failure to make a reasonable adjustment is considered in **Chapter 6** below.

Who has rights under the Act?

ss 1–2
Schs 1–2

2.9 An adult or child has protection from discrimination under the Act if he or she is a disabled person. A disabled person is someone who has a physical or mental impairment which has an effect on his or her ability to carry out normal day-to-day activities. That effect must be:

- substantial (that is, more than minor or trivial); and

- adverse; and

- long term (that is, it has lasted or is likely to last for at least a year or for the rest of the life of the person affected).

2.10 Physical or mental impairment includes sensory impairments. Hidden impairments are also covered (for example mental illness or mental health problems, learning disabilities and conditions such as diabetes or epilepsy). People who have had a disability within the terms of the Act in the past are protected from discrimination even if they no longer have the disability.

2.11 For a fuller understanding of the concept of disability under the Act, reference should be made to the **Appendix** to this Code. A Government publication, *Guidance on matters to be taken into account in determining questions relating to the definition of disability*, provides additional help in understanding the concept of disability and in identifying disabled persons (see paragraph 1.12 above). Where relevant, the *Guidance* must be taken into account in any legal proceedings.

What services are affected by Part III of the Act?

2.12 Under the Act, the provision of services includes the provision of goods or facilities (and in this Code "services" is used in this sense). Subject to the exclusions set out in paragraph 2.18 below, the Act affects everyone concerned with the provision in the United Kingdom of services to the public, or to a section of the public, whether in the private, public or voluntary sectors. It does not matter if services are provided free (such as access to a public park) or in return for payment (for example a meal in a restaurant). s 19(2)

2.13 Among the services which are covered are those provided to the public by local councils, Government departments and agencies, the emergency services, charities, voluntary organisations, hotels, restaurants, pubs, post offices, banks, building societies, solicitors, accountants, telecommunications and broadcasting organisations, public utilities (such as gas, electricity and water suppliers), national parks, sports stadia, leisure centres, advice agencies, theatres, cinemas, hairdressers, shops, market stalls, petrol stations, telesales businesses, places of worship, courts, hospitals and clinics. This list is for illustration only and does not cover all the services falling under the Act. s 19(3)

2.14 All those involved in providing services are affected – from the most senior director or manager to the most junior employee, whether full or part-time, permanent or temporary. It does not matter whether the services in question are being provided by a sole trader, a firm, company or other organisation, or whether the person involved in providing the services is self-employed or an employee, volunteer, contractor or agent.

2.15 It is important to remember that it is the provision of the service which is affected by Part III of the Act and not the nature of the service or business or the type of establishment from which it is provided.

> A bank is subject to Part III of the Act whenever and wherever it provides services to the public. For example, a bank providing its services from temporary or mobile premises during a two-week tennis tournament is still covered by the Act.

> A local leisure centre is subject to the Act because it provides a service to the public and not, for example, because its services are provided from a public building.

2.16 In some circumstances, the identity of the service provider who has liability under the Act may be unclear. This may happen where premises or facilities are shared by more than one business or organisation. It may also arise where a service appears to be provided by more than one service provider. In such a case it may be important to identify who is actually responsible for the provision of the service which has given rise to the alleged discrimination. In some cases, liability under the Act may be shared among a number of service providers.

> A bank provides a cash machine facility inside a supermarket. Although the facility is located on the supermarket's premises, the service is being provided by the bank. The bank is likely to be responsible for any duties that may arise under the Act in respect of the cash machine. However, the supermarket is likely to be responsible for ensuring that the cash machine is physically accessible to disabled customers using its premises.

An airport grants a franchise to a crèche to provide its services in a part of the airport. Although the crèche is located on the airport's premises, the service is being provided by the franchisee. The franchisee is likely to be responsible for any duties that may arise under the Act in respect of the crèche. However, access through the airport to the crèche is the responsibility of the airport.

A training company organises a conference to be held at a hotel. Although the conference is taking place at the hotel, the service in question is being provided by the training company. The conference organisers are likely to be responsible for any duties that may arise under the Act in respect of the conference. The company should ensure that the venue it chooses for the conference is accessible to disabled people. However, there may be some services which the hotel provides which are ancillary to the conference (for example, accommodation the night before the conference) and for which it is likely to be liable under the Act.

What services are not affected?

2.17 Part II of the Act exempts some employers according to the number of people they employ. There are no exemptions of this kind (whether relating to size, turnover or any other factor) for service providers under Part III.

2.18 Some services are excluded under Part III of the Act. These are:

s 19(5)

- **education** and some services which are very closely related to it (but see paragraph 2.19 below), such as:

  s 19(5)(a)

  - youth services provided by a local education authority;

  SI 1996/1836 reg 9

  - social, cultural and recreational activities and facilities for physical education and training designed to promote personal or educational development provided by a voluntary organisation (for example, a local branch of the scouts or guides);

  - some examination and assessment services; and

  - facilities for research students; and

- **the use of any means of transport**, although the transport infrastructure, for example, bus stations and airports, is covered (see paragraph 2.21).

Education

2.19 Although education is excluded from Part III of the Act, other non-educational services which are provided by a school, college or university on its premises are subject to the Act.

> A parent-teacher association holds a fund-raising event in a school hall. This is a provision of a service which is likely to be subject to the Act.

> A disabled student at a university is not protected by Part III if a lecture theatre is not accessible to her in the course of her studies because of her disability. But if the university offers the lecture theatre as a conference venue to outside organisations, this is a provision of a service which is likely to be subject to Part III.

> A college provides welfare and advice services to its students. This is a provision of a service which is likely to be subject to the Act.

2.20 The law requires schools, colleges and universities to provide information on access to education for disabled pupils and students. Other legislation makes provision for the education of disabled people.

Transport

2.21 Part III of the Act does not apply to any service so far as it consists of the use of any means of transport (for example, taxis, hire cars, buses, coaches, trains, aircraft and ships). However, this does not mean that transport providers are wholly exempt from Part III. They still have a duty to avoid discrimination against disabled people and to make reasonable adjustments for them in respect of matters like timetables, booking facilities, waiting rooms, etc, at airports, ferry terminals and bus, coach and rail stations.

A wheelchair user has no protection under Part III of the Act if a ferry on which he wishes to travel is not accessible. However, if he is refused service in the buffet bar of the ferry terminal because of his disability, this is likely to be unlawful.

2.22 Part V of the Act allows the Government to set access standards for buses, coaches, trains, trams and taxis. The Government has produced regulations on access standards for rail vehicles. Similar regulations are planned for buses, coaches and taxis.

SI 1998/2456
SI 1998/2457

Services not available to the public
Private clubs

2.23 Services not available to the public, such as those provided by private clubs, are not covered by Part III of the Act. However, where a club does provide services to the public then the Act applies to those services.

s 19(2)(b)

A private golf club refuses to admit a disabled golfer to membership. This is not covered by the Act. However, if the golf club hires out its facilities for a wedding reception, the Act applies to this service. If the club allows non-members to use the course, a refusal to allow a disabled golfer to play is likely to be subject to the Act.

2.24 Private clubs are generally those where membership is a condition of participation and members have to comply with a genuine process of selection, usually by a club committee operating the club rules. Private clubs may include special interest clubs, such as a film club or cricket club, or clubs for particular groups of people, such as military or political clubs. However, simply calling a service a "club" does not necessarily mean that the courts will consider it to be a private club. For example, commercially run businesses which may require membership – such as a health club or a video rental shop – would normally still be providing services to the public and, therefore, would be covered by the Act.

A health club in a hotel is open to the public. Club members pay an annual subscription and are provided with a membership card. Before using the club's fitness equipment, a member must undergo a fitness test. Although members have to satisfy certain requirements in order to use some of its facilities, compliance with a genuine selection procedure for membership is not a condition of using the club. The club is providing services to the public and is unlikely to be excluded from Part III of the Act.

Manufacturers and designers of products

2.25 The manufacture and design of products are not in themselves covered by Part III of the Act because they do not involve the provision of services direct to the public. Nothing in the Act requires manufacturers or designers to make changes to their products, packaging or instructions. However, it makes good business sense for manufacturers and designers to make their goods (and user information) more accessible to disabled customers and they should consider doing so as a matter of good practice.

A manufacturer of garden tools distributes its products only through high street shops. The Act does not require the manufacturer to design or market the goods so as to be easily useable by disabled purchasers.

2.26 However, if a manufacturer does provide services direct to the public, then it may have duties under the Act as a service provider.

A manufacturer of electrical goods provides a free guarantee. A purchaser of the goods is then entitled to have the goods replaced by the manufacturer if they are faulty within six months of purchase. For a fixed sum the manufacturer also provides an optional extended guarantee covering the goods against defects for up to two years after purchase. In both cases, the manufacturer is providing a service to the public (the guarantee) and is subject to the Act in relation to the provision of that service (but not in relation to the goods themselves).

A manufacturer of self-assembly furniture sells its products direct to the public by mail and telephone order and through a factory shop on its premises. It has duties under the Act because it is providing a service to the public. For example, it may have to make reasonable adjustments to the way in which it provides its service.

A food processing company produces tinned food which it supplies to a supermarket chain. Whether the tins are branded with the supermarket's own label or with that of the producer, the food processing company is not supplying goods to the public and so does not have duties under the Act. The supermarket is likely to have duties under the Act because it is supplying goods to the public, but these duties do not extend to the labelling or packaging of the tinned food.

3

The service provider's duty not to treat a disabled person less favourably

Introduction

3.1 This chapter addresses the duty of service providers to ensure that disabled people are not treated less favourably than other people when using their services. It explains what is made unlawful by the Act and what is meant by "less favourable treatment".

What is unlawful?

s 19(1) 3.2 The Act says that it is unlawful for a service provider to discriminate against a disabled person by:

s 19(1)(a) • refusing to provide (or deliberately not providing) any service which it offers or provides to members of the public; or

s 19(1)(c) • providing service of a lower standard or in a worse manner; or

s 19(1)(d) • providing service on worse terms; or

s 19(1)(b) • failing to comply with a duty to make reasonable adjustments (under section 21 ___ Act) if that failure has the effect of making it imposs___ unreasonably difficult for the disabled person to m___ e of any such service.

The consequences of a fail___ omply with a duty to make reasonable adjustments a___ idered in **Chapters 4 and 5**.

Less favourable treatment

s 20(1) 3.3 A service provider discriminates against a disabled person if, for a reason which relates to the disabled person's disability, it treats the disabled person less favourably than it treats (or would treat) others to whom that reason does not (or would not) apply and it cannot show that the treatment in question is justified. Whether and when a service provider might be able to **justify** the less favourable treatment of a disabled person is considered in **Chapter 6** below.

When is "less favourable treatment" unlawful discrimination?

3.4 For a disabled person to be discriminated against in this way, he or she must have been treated less favourably by a service provider in comparison with how the service provider treats (or would treat) other people. The reason for the less favourable treatment must relate to the disabled person's disability. The disability-related treatment of the disabled person is compared with how the service provider treats (or would treat) other people to whom the disability-related reason does not apply.

> A football club admits visiting supporters to its stadium. However, one visiting supporter is refused entry because he has cerebral palsy and has difficulty controlling and co-ordinating his movements. No other visiting supporter is refused entry. This would amount to less favourable treatment for a reason related to disability and, unless the football club can justify its actions, would be an unlawful refusal of service contrary to the Act.

3.5 Bad treatment is not necessarily the same as less favourable treatment although, where a service provider acts unfairly or inflexibly, a court might draw inferences that discrimination has occurred.

> All the supporters of a visiting team are refused entry to the stadium by the football club in the example in paragraph 3.4. A visiting supporter with cerebral palsy is being treated no differently from all the other visiting supporters. He has not been subjected to any less favourable treatment for a reason related to disability. However, if the football club refused entry to all the visiting supporters because one of their numbers has cerebral palsy, that could amount to unlawful discrimination against the disabled supporter.

3.6 The comparison can also be between the way in which one disabled person is treated compared to the way in which people with other disabilities are treated.

17

> The football club in the example in paragraph 3.4 refused entry to the disabled supporter with cerebral palsy. It cannot claim that it did not discriminate simply because people with other disabilities were allowed entry. The supporter with cerebral palsy has been less favourably treated in comparison with other members of the public, including the supporters with other disabilities.

3.7 A disabled person does not have to show that others were treated more favourably than they were. It is still less favourable treatment if others would have been treated better.

> A party of adults with learning disabilities has exclusively booked a restaurant for a special dinner. The restaurant staff spend most of the evening making fun of the party and provide it with worse service than normal. The fact that there are no other diners in the restaurant that evening does not mean that the disabled people have not been treated less favourably than other people. Other diners would not have been treated in this way.

3.8 There must be a connection between the less favourable treatment and a reason related to the disabled person's disability.

> A publican refuses to serve a disabled person whom he knows has epilepsy. He gives her no reason for refusing to serve her. Other customers in the pub are not refused service. A court is likely to draw an inference of discrimination in the absence of a reasonable explanation. However, if the ground for refusing her service is because she has no money, then the treatment is not for a reason which related to the disabled person's disability.

3.9 Treating a disabled person less favourably cannot be excused on the basis that another customer who behaved similarly would be treated in the same way.

> A group of deaf people who use British Sign Language (BSL) is refused entry to a disco. The doorman assumes that other customers might mistake communication using BSL as threatening gestures. This refusal of service is for a reason related to disability. It is likely to be unlawful even though the disco would have refused entry to any person who made threatening gestures.

3.10 Nevertheless, the Act cannot be used as a pretext for disruptive or anti-social behaviour unrelated to a person's disability.

> A disco ejects a person with an artificial arm because he has drunk too much and has become abusive and disorderly. The disco would have ejected any other patron in similar circumstances. The ejection (or refusal to serve) is not for a reason related to the disabled person's disability and is unlikely to be unlawful.

3.11 Unjustified less favourable treatment of a disabled person for a reason related to disability is unlawful when it results in a service provider:

- refusing to provide (or deliberately not providing) any service which it offers to the public; or

- providing service of a lower standard or in a worse manner; or

- providing service on worse terms.

See paragraph 3.2 above and paragraphs 3.12 to 3.17 immediately below.

Refusal or non-provision of service

3.12 A service provider cannot refuse to provide (or deliberately not provide) a service to a disabled person which it offers to other people, unless the refusal (or non-provision) can be justified. | s 19(1)(a)

> A party of disabled children is on a visit to a zoo. Without giving any explanation, the manager refuses to allow the children to enter the zoo. This is a refusal of a service and is likely to be unlawful.

> Bar staff in a pub pretend not to see a disabled person who is trying to be served at the bar. This is a non-provision of a service and is likely to be unlawful.

3.13 Although there is nothing unlawful about genuinely seeking to assist disabled people by informing them where they might get service more suited to their requirements, refusing to serve a disabled person may be unlawful whatever the intention or motive. For example, if a disabled person wishes to be served by a service provider, it cannot refuse to serve him or her simply on the ground that another service provider caters better for his or her requirements.

> An assistant in a small shop refuses to serve a disabled person, arguing that a nearby larger shop can offer a better service to disabled people. This is a refusal of service and is likely to be against the law.

3.14 Spurious reasons cannot be used to refuse to serve a disabled person – even if the service provider thinks that serving the disabled person will upset or raise objections from other customers.

> A disabled person with Tourette's syndrome (which causes him to utter obscenities involuntarily and compulsively) wishes to book a hotel room. The hotel receptionist pretends that all rooms are taken in order to refuse his booking because of his disability. This is likely to be against the law.

Standard or manner of service

s 19(1)(c) 3.15 A service provider must not offer a disabled person a lower standard of service than it offers other people or serve a disabled person in a worse manner, without justification. A lower standard of service might include harassment of disabled customers or being offhand or rude towards them.

> The manager of a fast-food outlet tells a person with a severe facial disfigurement that he must sit at a table out of sight of other customers, despite other tables being free. This is likely to be against the law.

3.16 A service provider does not have to stock special products for disabled people in order to avoid providing a worse standard of service (although as a matter of good practice it might consider doing so). However, if the service provider would take orders from other customers for products which it does not normally stock, it would be likely to be unlawful to refuse to take such an order from a disabled person.

> A disabled customer with a visual impairment wishes to buy a large print edition of a book from a bookshop. The bookshop does not stock large print books. This is not against the law. However, the disabled customer asks the bookshop to order a large print copy of the book. If the bookshop would usually take special orders from non-disabled customers, a refusal to accept the disabled customer's order is likely to be unlawful.

Terms of service

3.17 A service provider should not provide a service to a disabled person on terms which are worse than the terms offered to other people, without justification. Worse terms include charging more for goods or imposing extra conditions for using a service (but see paragraph 6.23 below). s 19(1)(d)

> A person who has Usher syndrome (and who, as a consequence, is deafblind) is booking a holiday. The travel agent asks her for a larger deposit than it requires from other customers. The travel agent believes, without good reason, that because of her disability she is more likely to cancel her holiday. This is likely to be against the law.

> A disabled customer who is partially sighted applies for a hire purchase loan from a finance company. The company is willing to lend to the customer, but on the condition that he should have his signature to the loan agreement witnessed by a solicitor. The company would not ask other borrowers to do this. This is likely to be unlawful.

Can service providers treat a disabled person more favourably?

3.18 The Act does not prohibit positive action in favour of disabled people (unless this would be unlawful under other legislation). Therefore, service providers may provide services on more favourable terms to a disabled person.

> A theatre manager offers a better seat in the theatre without extra charge to a person with a sight impairment who is accompanied by a guide dog. This is to allow room for his dog. This is within the law.

> A leisure park offers free entry to a communicator-guide accompanying a deafblind person. This allows the deafblind person to enjoy the park without having to pay two entrance fees. This is within the law.

Making changes for disabled people: the service provider's duty to make reasonable adjustments

Introduction

4.1 This chapter is concerned with the duty to make reasonable adjustments for disabled people. That duty is a cornerstone of the Act and requires service providers to take positive steps to make their services accessible to disabled people. This goes beyond simply avoiding treating disabled people less favourably for a disability-related reason.

s 21

What does the Act say?

4.2 One of the ways in which a service provider discriminates against a disabled person is where the service provider:

s 20(2)

- fails to comply with a duty to make reasonable adjustments imposed on it in relation to the disabled person; **and**

s 20(2)(a)

- cannot show that the failure to comply with that duty is justified.

s 20(2)(b)

Whether and when a service provider might be able to justify a failure to make a reasonable adjustment is considered in **Chapter 6** below.

4.3 It is unlawful for a service provider to discriminate in this way if the effect is to make it impossible or unreasonably difficult for the disabled person to make use of services which the service provider offers to the public.

s 19(1)(b)

What is the duty to make reasonable adjustments?

4.4 From 1 October 1999, where a service provider offers services to the public, it has a legal duty to take such steps as it is reasonable for the service provider to have to take in all the circumstances of the case in the three situations described immediately below. This duty is referred to in this Code as the duty to make reasonable adjustments.

s 21

4.5 A service provider may have to:

- change a **practice, policy or procedure** which makes it impossible or unreasonably difficult for disabled people to make use of services;

s 21(1)

• provide a reasonable **alternative method** of making services available to disabled people where a **physical feature** makes it impossible or unreasonably difficult for disabled people to make use of them;

• provide an **auxiliary aid or service** if it would enable (or make it easier for) disabled people to make use of services.

4.6 The duty to provide a service by a reasonable alternative method (referred to in paragraph 4.5 above) is only one element of the duty in relation to physical features. The Government intends that the other elements of the duty (which will require a service provider to remove or alter a physical feature of its premises or to provide a reasonable means of avoiding the physical feature) will not come into force until **2004**. However, it makes sense now for service providers to plan ahead by taking any opportunities which arise, or bringing forward plans, to make alterations to their premises to benefit disabled people **before 2004**.

To whom is the duty to make reasonable adjustments owed?

4.7 A service provider's duty to make reasonable adjustments is a duty owed to disabled people at large. It is not simply a duty that is weighed up in relation to each individual disabled person who wants to access a service provider's services. Disabled people are a diverse group with different requirements which service providers need to consider.

At what point does the duty to make reasonable adjustments arise?

4.8 Service providers should not wait until a disabled person wants to use a service which they provide before they give consideration to their duty to make reasonable adjustments. They should be thinking now about the accessibility of their services to disabled people. Service providers should be planning continually for the reasonable adjustments they need to make, whether or not they already have disabled customers. They should anticipate the requirements of disabled people and the adjustments that may have to be made for them. In many cases, it is appropriate to ask customers to identify whether they have any particular requirements and, if so, what adjustments may need to be made. Failure to anticipate the need for an adjustment may render it too late to comply with the duty to make the adjustment. Furthermore, it may not of itself provide a defence to a claim that it was reasonable to have provided one.

An invitation to the public to make submissions and to attend a public inquiry indicates that any reasonable adjustments will be made on request if this will assist disabled people to make submissions or to attend the inquiry. This helps to ensure that the public inquiry is accessible.

How long does the duty continue?

4.9 The duty to make reasonable adjustments is a continuing duty. Service providers should keep the duty constantly under review in the light of their experience with disabled people wanting to access their services. In this respect it is an evolving duty, and not something that needs simply to be considered once and once only, and then forgotten. For example, technological developments may provide new or better solutions to the problems of inaccessible services.

What is meant by "reasonable steps"?

4.10 Section 21 refers to a service provider being under a duty to take such steps as it is reasonable, in all the circumstances of the case, for it to have to take in order to make reasonable adjustments. The Act does not specify that any particular factors should be taken into account. What is a reasonable step for a particular service provider to have to take depends on all the circumstances of the case. It will vary according to:

s 21

- the type of services being provided;

- the nature of the service provider and its size and resources;

- the effect of the disability on the individual disabled person.

4.11 However, without intending to be exhaustive, the following are some of the factors which might be taken into account when considering what is reasonable:

- whether taking any particular steps would be effective in overcoming the difficulty that disabled people face in accessing the services in question;

- the extent to which it is practicable for the service provider to take the steps;

- the financial and other costs of making the adjustment;

- the extent of any disruption which taking the steps would cause;

- the extent of the service provider's financial and other resources;

- the amount of any resources already spent on making adjustments;

- the availability of financial or other assistance.

Customers in a busy post office are served by staff at a counter after queuing in line. A disabled customer with severe arthritis wishes to purchase a TV licence. He experiences great pain if he has to stand for more than a couple of minutes. Other customers would not expect to have to undergo similar discomfort in order to buy a TV licence. Thus, the post office's queuing policy makes it unreasonably difficult for the disabled person to use the service. Consideration will have to be given to how the queuing policy could be adjusted so as to accommodate the requirements of such disabled customers.

The post office staff could ask the customer to take a seat and then serve him in the same way as if he had queued. Alternatively, it might provide a separate service desk with seating for disabled customers. Depending on the size of the post office, these might be reasonable steps to have to take to adjust the queuing policy. However, it is not likely to be a reasonable step for the post office to send a member of staff to the disabled customer's home in order to sell him the TV licence. The time and expense involved would probably be an unreasonable use of the post office's resources, particularly in proportion to the degree of benefit to the disabled customer.

4.12 It is more likely to be reasonable for a service provider with substantial financial resources to have to make an adjustment with a significant cost than for a service provider with fewer resources. The resources available to the service provider as a whole are likely to be taken into account as well as other calls on those resources. Where the resources of the service provider are spread across more than one business unit or profit centre, the calls on them all are likely to be taken into account in assessing reasonableness.

4.13 Service providers should bear in mind that there are no hard and fast solutions. Action which may result in reasonable access to services being achieved for some disabled people may not necessarily do so for others. Equally, it is not enough for service providers to make some changes if they still leave their services impossible or unreasonably difficult for disabled people to use.

> The organiser of a large public conference provides British Sign Language (BSL) interpreters to allow deaf delegates to follow the conference. However, this does not assist delegates with a mobility impairment or visual disabilities to access the conference, nor does it help delegates with a hearing impairment who do not use BSL but who can lipread. The conference organiser will need to consider the requirements of these delegates also.

4.14 Similarly, a service provider will not have taken reasonable steps if it attempts to provide an auxiliary aid or service which in practice does not help disabled people to access the service provider's services. The way in which an auxiliary aid or service is provided may be just as important as the auxiliary aid or service itself.

> Despite providing British Sign Language (BSL) interpreters for deaf delegates who use BSL, the conference organiser fails to ensure that those delegates have the option to be seated near and in full view of the interpreters and in a well lit area. As a result, not all those delegates are able to follow the interpretation. The auxiliary service provided has not been effective in making the conference fully accessible to those deaf delegates.

4.15 If, having considered the issue thoroughly, there are genuinely no steps that it would be reasonable for a service provider to take, the service provider is unlikely to be in breach of the law if it makes no changes. This is so even if, as a result, disabled people are unable to use its services or are able to use them only with unreasonable difficulty.

What is "unreasonably difficult"?

4.16 It is unlawful for a service provider to discriminate against a disabled person in failing to comply with a duty to make reasonable adjustments when the effect of that failure is to make it impossible or **"unreasonably difficult"** for the disabled person to make use of services provided to the public. The Act does not define what is meant by "unreasonably difficult".

4.17 However, when considering if services are unreasonably difficult for disabled people to use, service providers should take account of whether the time, inconvenience, effort or discomfort entailed in using the service would be considered unreasonable by other people if they had to endure similar difficulties (see the example at paragraph 4.11 above).

What happens if the duty to make reasonable adjustments is not complied with?

s 19(1)(b)
s 20(2)
s 21(10)

4.18 A service provider must comply with the duty to make reasonable adjustments in order to avoid committing an act of unlawful discrimination. A disabled person is able to make a claim against a service provider if:

- the service provider fails to do what is required; and

- that failure makes it impossible or unreasonably difficult for that disabled person to access any services provided by the service provider to the public; and

- the service provider cannot show that such a failure is justified.

Reasonable adjustments in practice

5

Introduction

5.1 In Chapter 4 the Code outlines the concept of the duty to make reasonable adjustments and provides an overview of the legal principles which underpin it. In this chapter the Code explains and illustrates how the duty works in practice. There are currently three parts to the duty:

- changing practices, policies and procedures;

- providing reasonable alternative methods of providing services;

- providing auxiliary aids and services.

This chapter considers each in turn.

Practices, policies and procedures
What is the duty to change a practice, policy or procedure?

5.2 When a service provider is providing services to its customers, it will have established a particular way of doing this. Its practices (including policies and procedures) may be set out formally or may have become established informally or by custom. A service provider might have a practice which – perhaps unintentionally – makes it impossible or unreasonably difficult for disabled people to make use of its services.

5.3 In such a case, the service provider must take such steps as it is reasonable for it to have to take, in all the circumstances, to change the practice so that it no longer has that effect. This may simply mean instructing staff to waive a practice or amending a policy to allow exceptions or abandoning it altogether. Often, such a change involves little more than an extension of the courtesies which most service providers already show to their customers.

s 21(1)

A restaurant has a policy of refusing entry to male diners who do not wear a collar and tie. A disabled man who wishes to dine in the restaurant is unable to wear a tie because he has psoriasis (a severe skin complaint) of the face and neck. Unless the restaurant is prepared to waive its policy, its effect is to exclude the disabled customer from the restaurant. This is likely to be unlawful.

A video rental shop allows only people who can provide a driving licence as proof of their identity to become members. This automatically excludes some disabled people from joining because the nature of their disabilities prevents them from obtaining a driving licence (for example blind people or some people with epilepsy or mental health problems). The shop would be required to take reasonable steps to change this practice. It does so by being prepared to accept alternative forms of identification from its customers. This is likely to be a reasonable step for the shop to have to take.

What are practices, policies and procedures?

5.4 Practices, policies and procedures relate to the way in which a service provider operates its business or provides its services. This includes any requirements that it makes of its customers. In principle, the terms cover:

- what a service provider actually does (its **practice**);

- what a service provider intends to do (its **policy**);

- how a service provider plans to go about it (its **procedure**).

However, the three terms overlap and it is not always sensible to treat them as separate concepts.

A DIY superstore has a policy of not allowing dogs onto its premises. Members of staff are instructed to prevent anyone with a dog from entering the superstore. The "no dogs" policy is enforced in practice by this procedure. The policy makes it unreasonably difficult for disabled people accompanied by a guide dog to use the DIY superstore. The superstore has a duty to take such steps as are reasonable for it to have to take to avoid that effect and to make its services accessible to disabled people. It decides to amend its "no dogs" policy by allowing an exception for disabled people accompanied by a guide dog. This is likely to be a reasonable step for the superstore to have to take.

What are "reasonable steps" in relation to practices, policies and procedures?

5.5 The Act does not define what are "reasonable steps" for a service provider to have to take in order to change its practices. The kinds of factors which may be relevant are described in paragraphs 4.10 to 4.15 above.

5.6 The purpose of taking the steps is to ensure that the practice no longer has the effect of making it impossible or unreasonably difficult for disabled people to use a service. Where there is an adjustment that the service provider could reasonably put in place and which would make the service accessible, it is not sufficient for the service provider to take some lesser step which would not result in the service being accessible.

A medium-sized supermarket installs one extra-wide check-out lane intending it to be available to customers who are wheelchair users or accompanied by infants. However, that check-out lane is also designated as an express lane available only to shoppers with 10 or fewer items. The effect of this practice is to exclude wheelchair users from taking advantage of the accessible check-out unless they are making only a few purchases. It is likely to be a reasonable step for the supermarket to have to take to amend its practice by designating another check-out lane as the express lane.

5.7 What might be a reasonable adjustment for a service provider to have to take initially might be insufficient later in the light of its experience.

An out-of-town shopping centre amends its car-parking policy by designating car-parking spaces close to the entrance for use by disabled customers with an "orange badge" car parking concession permit. This is likely to be a reasonable step for the shopping centre to have to take at this point. However, non-disabled customers frequently use these spaces. In the light of this, simply making designated spaces available is no longer a reasonable adjustment because, in practice, it does not make the services of the centre accessible to disabled people. The shopping centre instructs the car park attendant and security patrol to monitor the use of the car park. This ensures that the designated spaces are used only by disabled customers. This is likely to be a reasonable step for the shopping centre to have to take in the circumstances then known to it.

5.8 A practice may have the effect of excluding or screening out disabled people from enjoying access to services. Or the practice may create a barrier or hurdle which makes it unreasonably difficult for disabled people to access the services. In such cases, unless the practice can be justified, a reasonable step for a service provider to have to take might be to abandon it entirely or to amend or modify it so that it no longer has that effect.

A town hall has procedures for the evacuation of the building in the event of a fire or emergency. Visitors are required to leave the building by designated routes. The emergency procedures are part of the way in which the town hall provides services to its visitors. It modifies the procedures (with the agreement of the local fire authority) to allow visitors with mobility impairments or sensory disabilities to be evacuated safely. This is likely to be a reasonable step for the town hall to have to take.

An hotel refurbishes a number of rooms on each floor which are fully accessible to disabled guests. However, the hotel's reservations system allocates rooms on a first-come, first-served basis as guests arrive and register. The effect is that on some occasions the specially refurbished rooms are allocated to non-disabled guests and late arriving disabled guests cannot be accommodated in those rooms. The hotel decides to change its reservation policy so that the accessible rooms are either reserved for disabled guests in advance or are allocated last of all. This is likely to be a reasonable step for the hotel to have to take.

Reasonable adjustments and the physical features of premises

5.9 The duty to make reasonable adjustments in relation to physical features does not at present require a service provider to take any action to remove or alter a physical feature of its premises or to provide a reasonable means of avoiding the physical feature. Those duties will be introduced in **2004**. Only the duty to provide a reasonable alternative method of making the services available to disabled people is in force from 1 October 1999.

> A public inquiry point is located on the third floor of a Government office building and is accessed by a flight of stairs. This makes it impossible or unreasonably difficult for some disabled people to get to it. People with a mobility disability or a mental health problem (like anxiety-related depression) may find using the stairs difficult. The service provider would not be expected at present to make physical alterations to its premises. When the remaining duties relating to physical features are introduced, it might be reasonable to install a lift or move the inquiry point to an accessible ground floor. It may be sensible to plan or make such changes now, especially if refurbishment is being planned in any event.

5.10 Before the duty to make reasonable adjustments to physical features is fully in force in **2004** it will be necessary to revise the guidance given in this Code of Practice.

What is the duty to provide a service by an alternative method?

5.11 Where a "physical feature" makes it impossible or unreasonably difficult for disabled people to make use of any service which is offered to the public, a service provider must take such steps as it is reasonable in all the circumstances of the case for it to have to take to provide a reasonable alternative method of making the service available to disabled people.

s 21(2)(d)

> In the example in paragraph 5.9 above, the Government department should consider what it could do to provide a reasonable alternative method of making its inquiry service accessible to disabled members of the public. For example, it might provide an auxiliary service in the form of a telephone inquiry line (see paragraph 5.15 below).

What is a "physical feature"?

5.12 The *Disability Discrimination (Services and Premises) Regulations 1999* make provision for various things to be treated as physical features. A "physical feature" includes:

s 21(2)
SI 1999/1191
regs 2–3

- any feature arising from the design or construction of a building on the premises occupied by the service provider;

- any feature on those premises of any approach to, exit from or access to such a building;

- any fixtures, fittings, furnishings, furniture, equipment or materials in or on such premises;

- any fixtures, fittings, furnishings, furniture, equipment or materials brought onto premises (other than those occupied by or on behalf of the service provider) in the course of (and for the purpose of) providing services to the public;

- any other physical element or quality of land comprised in the premises occupied by the service provider.

All these features are covered whether temporary or permanent. A building means an erection or structure of any kind.

What are "reasonable steps" in relation to provision of a service by an alternative method?

5.13 The kinds of factors which may be relevant in deciding what are reasonable steps for a service provider to have to take are described in paragraphs 4.10 to 4.15 above.

5.14 A reasonable alternative method of making a service available may involve the provision of an auxiliary aid or service (see paragraph 5.15 below).

A small self-service pharmacist's shop has goods displayed on high shelving separated by narrow aisles. These are physical features. The goods are not easily accessible to many disabled people. The shop decides to provide a customer assistance service. On request, a member of staff locates goods and brings them to the cash till for a disabled customer. This is likely to be a reasonable step for the shop to have to take.

A small hardware store is located in an old building with a narrow entrance at the top of a flight of stairs. The shop is willing to serve disabled people by bringing goods to the customer at the entrance to the building. This is likely to be a reasonable step for the store to have to take.

> A free public art gallery is accessible by a steep flight of stairs at its front entrance. This is a physical feature which makes it impossible or unreasonably difficult for visitors with a mobility impairment to enter the gallery. A side entrance for staff use only is fully accessible and always open. The gallery decides to allow disabled people to use this side entrance. This is likely to be a reasonable step for the gallery to have to take.

Auxiliary aids and services

What is the duty to provide auxiliary aids or services?

5.15 A service provider must take reasonable steps to provide auxiliary aids or services if this would enable (or make it easier for) disabled people to make use of any services which it offers to the public.

s 21(4)

What is an auxiliary aid or service?

5.16 The Act gives two examples of auxiliary aids or services: the provision of information on audio tape and the provision of a sign language interpreter.

s 21(4)

> A building society provides information about its savings accounts on an audio tape. A customer with a visual impairment can use the audio tape at home or in a branch to decide whether to open an account. This is an auxiliary aid.

> A social services department has a member of staff able to communicate with deaf clients using British Sign Language. This is an auxiliary service.

5.17 But these are only illustrations of the kinds of auxiliary aids or services which a service provider might need to consider. An auxiliary aid or service might be the provision of a special piece of equipment or simply extra assistance to disabled people from (perhaps specially trained) staff. In some cases a technological solution might be available. In any event, service providers should ensure that any auxiliary aids it provides are carefully chosen and properly maintained.

A large supermarket provides specially designed shopping baskets and trolleys which can be easily used by disabled shoppers in a wheelchair or with reduced mobility. It also provides electronic hand-held bar code readers with synthesised voice output which helps customers with a visual impairment to identify goods and prices. These are auxiliary aids which enable disabled shoppers to use the supermarket's services.

Disabled customers with a visual impairment or a learning disability may need assistance in a large supermarket to locate items on their shopping list. The supermarket instructs one of its employees to find the items for them. The supermarket is providing an auxiliary service which makes its goods accessible.

A petrol station decides that an assistant will help disabled people use the petrol pumps on request. It places a prominent notice at the pumps advertising this assistance and the hours it is available. This is an auxiliary service and is likely to be a reasonable step for the petrol station to have to take.

5.18 What is an appropriate auxiliary aid or service will vary according to the type of service provider, the nature of the services being provided, and the requirements of the disabled customers or potential customers. Auxiliary aids and services are not limited to aids to communication.

A community centre is accessible by two raised steps. It provides a suitably chosen portable temporary ramp which helps disabled people with a mobility impairment to enter the premises safely. This is an auxiliary aid which is suited to the requirements of those people.

A new cinema complex has deep airline-style seats. A disabled patron with restricted growth finds it difficult to see the screen when using such a seat. The cinema provides a bolster cushion on request which enables him to enjoy the film. This is an auxiliary aid appropriate to the circumstances.

A museum provides a written guide to its exhibits. It wants to make the exhibits accessible to visitors with learning disabilities. The museum produces a version of the guide which uses plain language, text and pictures to explain the exhibits. This is an auxiliary aid suited to visitors with learning disabilities and may also benefit other people.

5.19 *The Disability Discrimination (Services and Premises) Regulations 1999* made under the Act provide that (until the balance of the duties in relation to physical features comes into force in 2004) devices, structures or equipment, the installation, operation or maintenance of which would necessitate making a permanent alteration to (or which would have a permanent effect on) the physical fabric of premises, fixtures, fittings, furnishings, furniture, equipment or materials are not to be treated as auxiliary aids or services.

s 21(4)
SI 1999/1191
reg 4

5.20 This means that, at present, service providers are not required to do anything that would involve a permanent alteration to the physical fabric of premises (or fixtures, fittings, furnishings, furniture, equipment or materials) when providing an auxiliary aid. However, there is nothing in the Act to prevent service providers from making changes which do involve a permanent alteration when providing an auxiliary aid before the law changes in 2004, when such alterations will be required where reasonable. Indeed, it might be more effective and economical to adopt such an approach (see also paragraph 10.18 on good practice when providing auxiliary aids).

5.21 Nothing in the Act requires a service provider to provide an auxiliary aid or service to be used for personal purposes unconnected to the services being provided or to be taken away by the disabled person after use.

A solicitors' firm lends an audio tape recorder to a client with multiple disabilities who is unable to communicate in writing or to attend the firm's office. The client uses this auxiliary aid in order to record his instructions or witness statement. The client would be expected to return the recorder after use.

What are "reasonable steps" in relation to auxiliary aids or services?

5.22 The duty to provide auxiliary aids or services requires the service provider to take such steps as it is reasonable for it to have to take in all the circumstances of the case to make its services accessible to disabled people. What might be reasonable for a large service provider (or one with substantial resources) might not be reasonable for a smaller service provider.

A small family doctors' practice makes its surgery consultations more accessible to patients with speech or hearing impairments by using a pencil and notepad to communicate. This is likely to be a reasonable step for this practice to have to take. The size of the service provider, the resources available to it and the cost of the auxiliary service are relevant factors.

However, for a deaf patient who uses British Sign Language as his or her main form of communication, having a BSL interpreter would be an even more effective method of communication. This is because for people whose first language is BSL (rather than spoken or written English), exchange of written notes or lipreading can be an uncertain means of communication.

Using a BSL interpreter during a hospital appointment might be a reasonable step for a large hospital to have to take in some circumstances. This is likely to be a reasonable step to have to take when a consultant is explaining the implications of major surgery to a deaf patient who uses BSL as his or her main form of communication.

A small, private museum with limited resources provides a daily guided tour of its exhibits. It investigates the provision of a radio microphone system for hearing aid users to accompany the tour, but after careful consideration it rejects that option as expensive and impracticable. Instead, with very little effort or cost, the museum decides to provide good quality audio taped guides (with an option of plug-in neck loops) which can be used by persons with hearing aids who want to follow the guided tour. This is likely to be a reasonable step for the museum to have to take.

5.23 The reasonableness of the service provider's response to disabled people's requirements will inevitably vary with the circumstances. The kinds of factors which may be relevant are described in paragraphs 4.10 to 4.15 above.

The doctors' practice in the first example in paragraph 5.22 anticipates that there could be cases where a medical consultation with a deaf patient (who uses BSL as his or her main form of communication) would require the provision of a BSL interpreter. It is willing to provide such an auxiliary service when counselling about a life-threatening illness or explaining a decision as to whether surgery is necessary. This is likely to be a reasonable step for the practice to have to take in these circumstances.

5.24 British Sign Language interpretation may not be easily available, even if attempts are made to arrange it in advance. If this is the case, it may not be reasonable to provide an interpreter. The service provider will have to consider an alternative method of communication with a deaf person, if it is possible to do so. For example, many (but not all) deaf people are able to lipread.

5.25 A service provider will have to consider what steps it can reasonably take to meet the individual requirements of disabled people. How effectively a service provider is able to do so will depend largely on how far it has anticipated the requirements of its disabled customers. Many things that seem impossible at the time they are confronted might have been accommodated relatively easily if prior thought had been given to the question.

5.26 The Act leaves open what particular auxiliary aids or services might be provided in specific circumstances. Disabled people may be able to help the service provider to identify difficulties in accessing the service and what kind of auxiliary aid or service will overcome them. It is good practice to include disabled customers in the process of considering what reasonable adjustments should be made. However the duty remains on the service provider to determine what steps it needs to take.

Using auxiliary aids or services to improve communication

5.27 In many cases, a service provider will need to consider providing auxiliary aids or services to improve communication with people with a sensory impairment (such as those affecting hearing or sight) or a speech impairment or learning disabilities. The type of auxiliary aid or service will vary according to the importance, length, complexity or frequency of the communication involved. In some cases, more than one type of auxiliary aid or service might be appropriate, as different people have different communication requirements. Account should also be taken of people with multiple communication disabilities, such as deafblindness or combined speech and hearing disabilities.

> A cinema offers patrons a telephone booking service. Its booking office installs a textphone and trains its staff to use it. This offers access to deaf patrons and is likely to be a reasonable step for the cinema to have to take.

> The booking office of a small heritage railway decides to communicate with passengers who have speech or hearing impairments by exchanging written notes. This is likely to be a reasonable step for this service provider to have to take. However, it is unlikely to be a sufficient reasonable adjustment for the booking office at a large mainline rail terminus to make for such passengers. Instead, without altering the physical fabric of its premises, it installs an induction loop system and a textphone. These are likely to be reasonable steps for a large station to have to take.

Hearing disabilities

5.28 For people with hearing disabilities, the range of auxiliary aids or services which it might be reasonable to provide to ensure that services are accessible might include one or more of the following:

- written information (such as a leaflet or guide);

- a facility for taking and exchanging written notes;

- a verbatim speech-to-text transcription service;

- non-permanent induction loop systems;

- subtitles;

- videos with sign language interpretation;

- information displayed on a computer screen;

- accessible Websites;

- textphones, telephone amplifiers and inductive couplers;

- teletext displays;

- audio-visual telephones;

- audio-visual fire alarms (not involving physical alterations to premises);

- qualified sign language interpreters or lipspeakers.

A deaf defendant (or defender) in court proceedings uses BSL as his main form of communication. The court arranges for a qualified BSL interpreter (familiar with legal procedure and terminology) to interpret and voice over his evidence in court. This is likely to be a reasonable step for the court to have to take.

A hearing impaired person who lipreads as her main form of communication wants a secured loan from a bank. In the initial stages it might be reasonable for the bank to communicate with her by providing printed literature or information displayed on a computer screen. However, before a secured loan agreement is signed, this particular bank usually provides a borrower with a verbal explanation of its contents. At that stage it might be reasonable, with the customer's consent, for the bank to arrange for a lipspeaker to be present so that any complex aspects of the agreement can be fully explained and communicated.

A television broadcasting company provides teletext sub-titles to some of its programmes. This allows viewers with a hearing impairment to follow the programmes more easily. This is likely to be a reasonable step for the broadcasting company to have to take.

5.29 Where sign language interpretation is used as an auxiliary service, it is important for the interpreter to use the same sign language system as the deaf person. The interpreter should be capable of communicating accurately and efficiently with both the disabled person and the other parties involved.

5.30 Service providers should bear in mind that hearing impairments take many forms and are of varying degrees. What might be a reasonable auxiliary aid or service for a person with tinnitus or reduced hearing might not be a reasonable adjustment for someone who is profoundly deaf.

> A bus station fits a temporary induction loop system at its booking office. This ensures that customers who have reduced hearing and use hearing aids are able to communicate effectively with the booking office. However, this does not help profoundly deaf customers. The bus company instructs its staff to take time to communicate by using a pen and notepad to discover what the customer wants and to give information. The staff are also trained to speak looking directly at the customer to allow those customers who can lipread to do so. These are likely to be reasonable steps for the bus station to have to take.

Visual impairments

5.31 For people with visual impairments, the range of auxiliary aids or services which it might be reasonable to provide to ensure that services are accessible might include one or more of the following:

- readers;

- documents in large or clear print, Moon or Braille;

- information on computer diskette;

- information on audiotape;

- telephone services to supplement other information;

- spoken announcements or verbal communication;

- accessible Websites;

- assistance with guiding;

- audiodescription services;
- large print or tactile maps/plans and three-dimensional models;
- touch facilities.

> A restaurant changes its menus daily. For that reason it considers it is not practicable to provide menus in alternative formats, such as Braille. However, its staff spend a little time reading out the menu for blind customers and the restaurant ensures that there is a large print copy available. These are likely to be reasonable steps for the restaurant to have to take.

> A utility company supplying gas and electricity to domestic customers sends out quarterly bills. On request, the company is willing to provide the bills in alternative formats such as Braille or large print for customers with visual impairments. This is likely to be a reasonable step for the utility company to have to take.

> Every year a local council sends out information to local residents about new council tax rates. Because the information is important, the council provides copies in large print. On request, it is also prepared to supply the information in alternative media such as Braille or audiotape or to provide a verbal explanation of the new rates to individual residents with visual impairments. These are likely to be reasonable steps for the council to have to take.

> A customer with a visual impairment wishes to buy a compact disc player from a small specialist hi-fi shop. The shop arranges for a member of staff to assist the customer by reading out product details, packaging information or prices. This is likely to be a reasonable step for the shop to have to take.

5.32 As with other forms of sensory impairments, visual disabilities are of varying kinds and degrees. Service providers need to consider what is the most appropriate auxiliary aid or service to provide. More than one auxiliary aid or service may be necessary according to the circumstances.

A small estate agent is reviewing the accessibility of its sales literature for clients who are partially sighted or blind. Because of the nature of the service it provides and the size of its business, the estate agent concludes that it is not practicable to make particulars of houses for sale available in Braille. However, the estate agent decides to change the print size and redesign the appearance of its written sales particulars. This makes the estate agent's sales information more accessible to its partially sighted clients, but does not assist those who are blind. It therefore also decides to put the information on audio tape on request. These are likely to be reasonable steps for the estate agent to have to take.

A social security office ensures that claim forms and information literature are available in large print for partially sighted claimants. It also arranges for the forms and literature to be provided in Braille or on audiotape on request. These are likely to be reasonable steps for the social security office to have to take.

Other disabilities and multiple disabilities

5.33 There are many examples of how auxiliary aids or services can be used to improve communication with people who have hearing disabilities or visual impairments. Service providers should also consider how communication barriers can be overcome for people with other disabilities. For example, a customer with a learning disability may be able to access a service by the provision of documents in large, clear print and plain language or by the use of colour coding and illustrations.

A coach company issues its staff at a ticket office with a card showing destinations, types of tickets and prices. It trains the staff so that customers with learning disabilities can point to or ask for the options on the card that they want. These are likely to be reasonable steps for the coach company to have to take.

5.34 Service providers should not assume that their services are made accessible to customers with multiple disabilities simply by providing auxiliary aids or services which are suitable for people with individual disabilities.

5.35 For example, deafblind people (individuals who have a severe combined sight and hearing impairment) are not necessarily assisted in accessing services by the simple provision of communication aids designed for use by people with hearing disabilities or visual impairments. Such aids could assist deafblind people if appropriately used (for example information leaflets produced in Braille or Moon, good lighting and acoustics, induction loop systems, etc). However, what is appropriate will depend on the nature and extent of the individual's dual sensory impairment and the methods he or she uses to communicate and access information. Adjustments which may be of assistance to a deafblind person might include engaging a deafblind manual interpreter for important meetings or having a member of staff trained in specific ways to help a deafblind person. Where service providers give their staff disability awareness training, they should consider including ways of helping deafblind people, such as guiding them safely and tracing capital letters and numbers on the palm of the hand.

A branch of a bank with a regular deafblind customer has a particular staff member trained in communicating with deafblind people. At the customer's request, the bank arranges for statements and letters to be sent in Braille. These are likely to be reasonable steps for the bank to have to take.

Can a service provider justify less favourable treatment or failure to make reasonable adjustments?

Introduction

6.1 A service provider should not be looking for reasons or excuses to discriminate against disabled people who wish to use its services. It is in the service provider's own best interests to ensure that its services are fully accessible to all customers, regardless of disability.

6.2 However, in limited circumstances, the Act does permit a service provider to justify the less favourable treatment of a disabled person or a failure to make a reasonable adjustment. This cannot be used as a reason for a general exclusion of disabled people from access to services. The circumstances in which such treatment or failure might be justified are examined in this chapter.

6.3 Two further questions are also considered in this chapter – whether any additional costs of making adjustments can be passed on to disabled people and whether a service provider is obliged to make adjustments that affect the fundamental nature of its business or services (see paragraphs 6.24 – 6.26 below). There are also special rules affecting the provision of insurance, guarantees and deposits (these are dealt with in **Chapter 7** below).

Less favourable treatment

6.4 A service provider discriminates against a disabled person if:

s 20(1)(a)
- for a reason which relates to the disabled person's disability, it treats him or her less favourably than it treats or would treat others to whom that reason does not or would not apply; **and**

s 20(1)(b)
- it cannot show that the treatment in question is **justified**.

Failure to make reasonable adjustments

6.5 A service provider also discriminates against a disabled person if:

- it fails to comply with a duty to make reasonable adjustments imposed on it under the Act in relation to the disabled person; **and**

  s 20(2)(a)

- it cannot show that the failure to comply with that duty is **justified**.

  s 20(2)(b)

6.6 Treating a disabled person less favourably for a reason related to disability or failing to comply with a duty to make reasonable adjustments may be justified **only if**:

  s 20(9)

- the service provider believes that one or more of the relevant conditions detailed in paragraphs 6.10 to 6.23 below are satisfied; **and**

  s 20(3)(a

- it is reasonable in all the circumstances of the case for that person to hold that opinion.

  s 20(3)(b)

The general approach to justification

6.7 The test of justification is both subjective (what did the service provider believe?) and objective (was that belief reasonably held?). A service provider does not have to be an expert on disability, but it is expected to take account of all the circumstances, including the information available to it, whether it was possible to seek advice, and whether the service provider asked for and took account of the opinion of the disabled person concerned. The lawfulness of what a service provider does or fails to do will be judged by what it knew (or could reasonably have known), what it did and why it did it **at the time** of the alleged discriminatory act.

6.8 In some instances, it will not be clear whether any of the justifications apply. It may be shown subsequently that a service provider was mistaken in its opinion in a particular case. Coming to an incorrect conclusion does not necessarily mean that the service provider has discriminated unlawfully against a disabled person. In such cases, a service provider may be able to justify less favourable treatment or a failure to make reasonable adjustments if it can show that it was reasonable, in all the circumstances of the case, for it to hold that opinion at the time.

6.9 If a disabled person can show that he or she has been treated less favourably than others for a reason related to his or her disability, it is for the service provider to show that the

47

action taken was justified. Similarly, if a disabled person can show that the service provider has failed to comply with a duty to make reasonable adjustments in relation to the disabled person, it is for the service provider to show that the failure was justified. In either case, the justification must fall within one of the relevant categories of justification set out in the Act and which are described in paragraphs 6.10 to 6.23 immediately below.

Health or safety

s 20(4)(a)
s 20(9)

6.10 The Act does not require a service provider to do anything which would endanger the health or safety of any person. A service provider can justify less favourable treatment or a failure to make an adjustment if it is necessary in order not to endanger the health or safety of any person, including the disabled person in question.

> An amusement park operator refuses to allow a person with muscular dystrophy onto a physically demanding, high speed ride. Because of her disability, the disabled person uses walking sticks and cannot stand unaided. The ride requires users to brace themselves using their legs. The refusal is based on genuine concerns for the health or safety of the disabled person and other users of the ride. This is likely to be justified.

6.11 However, spurious health or safety reasons provide no defence. For example, fire regulations should not be used as an excuse to place unnecessary restrictions on disabled people. It is for the management of the establishment concerned, with advice from the licensing authority or local fire officer, to make any special provision needed. Service providers should avoid using safety requirements as an excuse for making discriminatory decisions based on stereotyping of disabled people or making generalisations or assumptions about them.

> Although there are adequate means of escape, a cinema manager turns away a wheelchair user because she unreasonably assumes, without checking, that he could be in danger in the event of a fire. This is unlikely to be justified.

48

> A sports stadium refuses entry to an unaccompanied blind person because the stadium management wrongly and unreasonably assumes that she will be a safety risk if the stadium has to be evacuated in an emergency. This is unlikely to be justified.

6.12 Before a service provider relies on health or safety to justify less favourable treatment of a disabled person, it should consider whether a reasonable adjustment could be made which would allow the disabled person to access the service without concerns for health or safety (for example, by amending an evacuation procedure). Similarly, if health or safety is used to justify a failure to make a particular reasonable adjustment, the service provider should consider whether there is any alternative adjustment that could be made to allow the disabled person to use the service.

> An outdoor venture centre provides management training weekends involving strenuous physical effort and some personal risk. On safety grounds, it has a policy of requiring its clients to undergo a medical examination before they are admitted to the course. This tends to screen out clients who are disabled as a result of high blood pressure or heart conditions. This is likely to be justified. However, the venture centre might make adjustments to its policy by admitting the disabled clients to any parts of the course which do not create a safety risk.

Incapacity to contract

6.13 The Act does not require a service provider to contract with a disabled person who is incapable of entering into a legally enforceable agreement or of giving an informed consent. If a disabled person is unable to understand a particular transaction, a service provider may refuse to enter into a contract. This might also justify discriminatory standards or manner or terms of service, as well as a failure to make a reasonable adjustment.

s 20(4)(b)
s 20(9)

6.14 Any such refusal must be reasonable. A person may be able to understand less complicated transactions, but have difficulty with more complex ones. Unless there is clear evidence to the contrary, a service provider should assume that a disabled person is able to enter into any contract.

A jeweller refuses to sell a pair of earrings to a person with a learning disability. It claims that she does not understand the nature of the transaction. This is even though her order is clear and she is able to pay for the earrings. This is unlikely to be justified.

A person with senile dementia applies for a mortgage loan from a building society to finance the purchase of a house. Although he has the means of keeping up with the mortgage loan repayments, the building society has sound reasons for believing that the disabled person does not understand the nature of the legal agreement and obligations involved. The building society refuses his application. This is likely to be justified.

A long-term patient in a psychiatric hospital wishes to open a bank account. The bank wrongly assumes that because she is in a hospital she is incapable of managing her affairs. It refuses to open an account unless it is provided with an enduring power of attorney. The bank continues with its refusal despite being provided with good evidence that the person has full capacity to manage her own affairs. This is unlikely to be justified.

SI 1996/1836
reg 8

6.15 *The Disability Discrimination (Services and Premises) Regulations 1996* made under the Act prevent service providers from justifying less favourable treatment of a disabled person on the ground of incapacity to contract or inability to give an informed consent where another person is legally acting on behalf of the disabled person. For example, that other person may be acting under a power of attorney (or, in Scotland, under a power exercisable in relation to the disabled person's property or affairs by a curator bonis, tutor or judicial factor).

A salesman refuses to rent a television to a woman simply because she is legally acting on behalf of her son who has a mental health problem. This is less favourable treatment of the son and is unlikely to be justified.

6.16 Before a service provider seeks to justify any form of discrimination against a disabled person on the ground of incapability of entering into an enforceable agreement or of giving an informed consent, the service provider should consider whether a reasonable adjustment could be made to solve this problem. For example, it might be possible to prepare a contractual document in plain English to overcome an inability to give an informed consent.

Service provider otherwise unable to provide the service to the public

6.17 A service provider can justify refusing to provide (or deliberately not providing) a service to a disabled person if this is necessary because the service provider would otherwise be unable to provide the service to other members of the public.

s 20(4)(c)

> A tour guide refuses to allow a person with a severe mobility impairment on a tour of old city walls because he has well-founded reasons to believe that the extra help the guide would have to give her would prevent the party from completing the tour. This is likely to be justified.

6.18 However, refusing service to a disabled person is only justifiable if other people would be effectively prevented from using the service at all unless the service provider treated the disabled person less favourably than other people. It is not enough that those other people would be inconvenienced or delayed.

> Disabled customers with a speech impairment or a learning disability may have difficulty in explaining to a bank cashier what their service requirements are. If the cashier asks the disabled customers to go to the back of the queue so as not to delay other customers waiting to be served, this is unlikely to be justified.

6.19 Before a service provider seeks to rely on this justification for a refusal of provision (or a non-provision) of services to a disabled person, it should first consider whether there are any reasonable adjustments that could be made to allow the disabled person to enjoy the service.

In the example in paragraph 6.17 above, the tour guide might consider whether an additional guide could be provided without fundamentally changing the nature of the service (see paragraph 6.25 below). This would be an example of an auxiliary service and might be a reasonable step for the tour guide to have to take.

To enable the service provider to provide the service

s 20(4)(d)   6.20   A service provider can justify providing service of a lower standard or in a worse manner or on worse terms (an inferior service) if this is necessary in order to be able to provide the service to the disabled person or other members of the public.

A hotel restricts a wheelchair user's choice of bedrooms to those with level access to the lifts. Those rooms tend to be noisier and have restricted views. The disabled person would otherwise be unable to use the hotel. The restriction is necessary in order to provide the service to the disabled guest. This is likely to be justified.

6.21   However, providing an inferior service to a disabled person is only justifiable if other people or the disabled person would be effectively prevented from using the service at all unless the service provider treated the disabled person less favourably than other people. A service provider cannot justify such treatment of a disabled person simply because of other people's preferences or prejudices.

A public fitness centre restricts the times a customer who has AIDS is allowed to use its facilities. The other users have objected to his presence and use of the centre's facilities because of a groundless fear that they might become infected with HIV by normal contact with him. Despite his reassurances, the centre has bowed to the pressure of the other customers. This is unlikely to be justified.

6.22 Before a service provider seeks to rely on this justification for an inferior service to a disabled person, it should first consider whether there are any reasonable adjustments that could be made to allow the disabled person to enjoy the service.

Greater expense

6.23 A service provider can justify charging a disabled person more for some services than it charges other people. This is where the service is individually tailored to the requirements of the disabled customer. If a higher charge reflects the additional cost or expense of meeting the disabled person's specification, that would justify the higher charge.

s 20(4)(e)

> A furniture shop charges more for an orthopaedic bed, made to the disabled customer's specification, than it does for a standard bed. This is likely to be justified.

Additional cost of providing the service

6.24 The Act does not allow a service provider to pass on the additional costs of complying with the duty to make reasonable adjustments to disabled customers alone. Reasonable adjustments form part of the service provider's general expenses of providing the service. Any increased cost in providing services to a disabled person – resulting from compliance with a duty to make reasonable adjustments – cannot be used to justify any difference in the terms on which a service is provided to a disabled person.

s 20(5)

> A guest house has installed an audio-visual fire alarm in one of its guest bedrooms in order to accommodate visitors with a sensory impairment. In order to recover the costs of this installation, the landlady charges disabled guests a higher daily charge for that room, although it is otherwise identical to other bedrooms. This is unlikely to be justified.

> A store provides a home delivery service for its customers. It charges for this service. It can therefore charge a disabled customer. However, there is nothing to prevent the store from waiving the charge for disabled customers and it might wish to do so as a matter of good practice.

Protecting the fundamental nature of a business or service

s 21(6)

6.25 The Act does not require a service provider to take any steps which would fundamentally alter the nature of its service, trade, profession or business. This means that a service provider does not have to comply with a duty to make reasonable adjustments in a way which would so alter the nature of its business that the service provider would effectively be providing a completely different kind of service.

> A restaurant refuses to deliver a meal to the home of a disabled person with severe agoraphobia (a fear of public or open spaces) on the grounds that this would result in the provision of a different kind of service. This is unlikely to be against the law. However, if the restaurant already provides a home delivery service, it is likely to be discriminatory to refuse to serve the disabled person in this way.

> A night club with low level lighting is not required to adjust the lighting to accommodate customers who are partially sighted if this would fundamentally change the atmosphere or ambience of the club.

> A bowling alley provides a simple portable bowling ramp to assist a disabled bowler to launch the bowl at the pins. That is likely to be a reasonable adjustment. However, the bowling alley is not required to alter the rules of the game, even if this could assist the disabled bowler to enjoy the facility even more.

> A hair and beauty salon provides appointments to clients at its premises in a town centre. A disabled person with a respiratory impairment is unable to travel into town because this exacerbates her disability. She asks the salon to provide her with an appointment at home. The salon refuses as it does not provide a home appointment service to any of its clients. This is likely to be within the law.

6.26 However, there might be an alternative reasonable adjustment which would ensure the accessibility of the services. If this can be provided without fundamentally altering the nature of the services or business, it would be a reasonable step for the service provider to have to take.

Special rules affecting insurance, guarantees and deposits

Introduction

7.1 There are special rules affecting the provision of particular services. The services in question are:

- insurance;

- guarantees;

- deposits in respect of goods and facilities.

This chapter addresses these special rules.

Insurance
When is disability relevant to the provision of insurance services?

SI 1996/1836

7.2 In some circumstances, the fact that a person is disabled may be a relevant factor in deciding whether to provide insurance services (including life assurance) to that person and, if so, on what terms. The *Disability Discrimination (Services and Premises) Regulations 1996* (the Regulations) made under the Act provide special rules to deal with those circumstances.

reg 2(1)

7.3 The special rules on insurance only apply to the provision of insurance services by an insurer. They are relevant where a provider of insurance services:

- for a reason which relates to a disabled person's disability

- treats a disabled person less favourably

- than it treats (or would treat) others to whom that reason does not (or would not) apply.

A disabled person with a history of cancer applies for a life insurance policy. The insurance company refuses to provide life insurance to her. Whether the refusal of insurance is justified will depend on the application of the special rules on insurance services.

> A disabled person with diabetes applies to a motor insurer for comprehensive insurance on his motor car. The insurer is willing to provide insurance cover to the disabled person but, because of his disability, only at a higher premium than would be charged to other motorists. Whether the less favourable terms on which the insurance cover is provided are justified will depend on the application of the special rules on insurance services.

7.4   The special rules state that disability-related less favourable treatment in the provision of insurance services is deemed to be justified if **all** the following conditions are satisfied:

reg 2(2)

- it is in connection with insurance business carried on by the service provider;

- it is based on information which is relevant to the assessment of the risk to be insured;

- the information is from a source on which it is reasonable to rely;

- the less favourable treatment is reasonable having regard to the information relied on and any other relevant factors.

> In the first example in paragraph 7.3 above, the insurer has based its refusal of life insurance on clear medical evidence from a cancer specialist that the disabled person is unlikely to live for more than six months. In the circumstances, the refusal of insurance is likely to be justified because all the conditions above are satisfied.

> A person with a diagnosis of manic depression applies for motor insurance. He is told that he will have to pay double the normal premium because of his condition. The insurer is relying on actuarial data relating to the risks posed by a person driving when in a manic episode. However, the applicant produces credible evidence that he has been stable on medication for some years and has an unblemished driving record. In these circumstances, the charging of a higher premium in this case is unlikely to be justified because not all of the conditions above have been fully satisfied.

What is information relevant to the assessment of an insurance risk?

reg 2(2)(b)

7.5 Information which might be relevant to the assessment of the risk to be insured includes actuarial or statistical data or a medical report. The information must also be current and from a source on which it is reasonable to rely. An insurer cannot rely on untested assumptions or stereotypes or generalisations in respect of a disabled person.

> In the second example in paragraph 7.3 above, if the motor insurer has based its decision to charge an increased premium on sound medical evidence and reliable statistical data, it is likely to be able to justify the increased premium.

What is the practical effect of the special rules on insurance?

7.6 An insurer should not adopt a general policy or practice of refusing to insure disabled people or people with particular disabilities unless this can be justified by reference to the four conditions set out in paragraph 7.4 above. Similarly, unless justifiable in this way, an insurer should not adopt a general policy or practice of only insuring disabled people or people with particular disabilities on additional or adverse terms or conditions.

> A private health insurer is considering an application for private health insurance from a disabled person with chronic bronchitis and emphysema. The insurer is willing to provide health insurance to her, but on the condition that claims resulting from respiratory illnesses are excluded from cover. That decision is based on relevant and reliable medical evidence relating to the individual applicant for insurance. This is likely to be reasonable and therefore justified.

7.7 The special rules on insurance services recognise that insurers may need to distinguish between individuals when assessing the risks which are the subject of an insurance proposal or insurance policy. However, it is for the insurer to show that there is an additional risk associated with a disabled person which arises from his or her disability. Blanket assumptions should be avoided.

Existing insurance policies, cover documents and master policies

7.8 The Regulations provide for insurance policies which existed before the Regulations came into force on 2 December 1996. Any less favourable treatment of a disabled person which results from such a policy is treated as automatically justified until the policy falls for renewal or review on or after 2 December 1996. Once renewed or reviewed, the policy falls within the special rules above.

reg 3

Guarantees

7.9 Manufacturers and service providers frequently give their customers guarantees in respect of goods, facilities or services. The Regulations contain special rules in respect of guarantees.

7.10 The special rules deal with situations where a disabled person's disability results in higher than average wear or tear to goods or services supplied and where it would not be reasonable to expect service providers to honour a guarantee.

reg 5

What is a guarantee?

7.11 A guarantee includes any document (however described) by which a service provider provides that:

reg 5(3)

- the purchase price of goods, facilities or services provided will be refunded if they are not of satisfactory quality; or

reg 5(2)(a)(i)

- services in the form of goods provided will be replaced or repaired if not of satisfactory quality.

reg 5(2)(a)(ii)

It does not matter whether the guarantee is legally enforceable.

reg 5(2)(a)

> A double-glazing firm gives customers a document described as a "Warranty". The document promises to refund the purchase price of the double-glazing within six months if the customer is not completely happy with their quality. This is a guarantee.

A manufacturer of telephones and answer machines distributes its products to high street stores. The high street stores sell the products to their customers. In the product packaging there is a card from the manufacturer promising to replace or repair its products free of charge if defective within one year of purchase. The card has to be completed and returned to the manufacturer by the purchaser. This is a guarantee.

A retail chain of stores undertakes to replace goods if they wear out or break within three months of purchase. Although this practice is not contained in a formal document and might not be legally enforceable, it is likely to be a guarantee.

Guarantees and less favourable treatment of disabled persons

reg 5(1)

7.12 The Regulations deal with the question of less favourable treatment of disabled people in respect of guarantees. The special rules apply where, in respect of a guarantee, a service provider:

- for a reason which relates to a disabled person's disability

- treats a disabled person less favourably

- than it treats (or would treat) others to whom that reason does not (or would not) apply.

reg 5(2)

7.13 Less favourable treatment of a disabled person in respect of a guarantee may be justified if **all** the following conditions are satisfied:

- the service provider has provided a guarantee (as explained in paragraph 7.11 above);

- damage has occurred for a reason which relates to the disabled person's disability;

- the service provider refuses to provide a replacement, repair or refund under the guarantee;

- that refusal is because the damage is above the level at which the guarantee would normally be honoured;

- the refusal is reasonable in all the circumstances of the case.

A disabled person with a mobility impairment buys a pair of shoes from the retail chain of stores in the third example in paragraph 7.11 above. He wears out the left shoe after a few months because his left foot has to bear most of his weight. The store refuses to provide a new pair of shoes because the old pair has undergone abnormal wear and tear. This is likely to be justified.

A wheelchair user has ordered a new front door from the double-glazing firm in the first example in paragraph 7.11 above. Despite being properly installed, within a few weeks the door is marked, scuffed and misaligned. This is because, as she enters and leaves her house, the customer's wheelchair regularly catches the door. The customer is unhappy because the firm specifically stated that the door would be able to withstand contact with her wheelchair. The double-glazing firm refuses to refund the purchase price on the ground that this represents abnormal wear and tear. In the light of the firm's express statement, this is unlikely to be justified.

Deposits

7.14 A service provider may be prepared to provide goods or facilities for hire or rent or on a "sale or return" basis. The customer is then often required to pay a deposit which is refundable if the goods or facilities are returned undamaged. The Regulations provide special rules to deal with the question of whether the service provider can refuse to return the deposit in full if damage has occurred to the goods or facilities because of the customer's disability or a reason related to it.

reg 6

7.15 The special rules apply where, in relation to a deposit, a service provider:

reg 6(1)

- for a reason which relates to a disabled person's disability

- treats a disabled person less favourably

- than it treats (or would treat) others to whom that reason does not (or would not) apply.

7.16 Less favourable treatment of a disabled person in respect of a deposit may be justified if **all** the following conditions are satisfied:

- the service provider has provided goods or facilities;

- the disabled person is required to provide a deposit;

- the deposit is refundable if the goods or facilities are undamaged;

- damage has occurred to the goods or facilities for a reason which relates to the disabled person's disability;

- the service provider refuses to refund some or all of the deposit;

- that refusal is because the damage is above the level at which the service provider would normally refund the deposit in full;

- the refusal is reasonable in all the circumstances of the case.

A disabled person hires an evening suit from a menswear hire shop. The hire shop requires all customers to pay a deposit against damage to the hired clothing. Because of the nature of his disability, the disabled person wears a leg calliper. This causes abnormal wear and tear to the suit. When the suit is returned, the hire shop retains part of the deposit against the cost of repairing the damage. This is likely to be justified.

7.17 The special rules on deposits do not justify a service provider charging a disabled person a higher deposit than it would charge to other people. Similarly, a service provider is not justified in charging a disabled person a deposit where the service provider would not expect other people to pay such a deposit. In either case, this could amount to discrimination in the terms on which goods or facilities are provided to the disabled person.

7.18 Where a service provider requires a disabled person to pay a deposit, it may only refuse to repay the deposit if any damage to the goods or facilities is above the level at which the service provider would normally refund the deposit in full. If the damage is of a level where the service provider would normally repay the deposit in full, a disabled person must not be treated less favourably than any other person who has paid a deposit and has caused comparable damage to the goods or facilities.

reg 6(2)(b)

7.19 A refusal to refund a deposit to a disabled person must be reasonable in all the circumstances of the case. A service provider is unlikely to be justified in withholding the whole or part of a deposit if the amount withheld exceeds the loss suffered by the service provider as a result of the damage.

reg 6(2)(c)

8

Selling, letting or managing premises

Introduction

ss 22–24   8.1   The Act makes it unlawful for landlords and other persons to discriminate against disabled people in the disposal or management of premises in certain circumstances. Such persons may also have duties as service providers where they are providing services to the public. Those duties have been discussed in the preceding chapters. This chapter explains the particular responsibilities that apply to landlords and other persons when selling, letting or managing premises. Such persons may include a legal entity such as a company, but, for convenience, they are referred to in this chapter as "he or she".

What does the Act make unlawful?

s 22(1)   8.2   It is unlawful for a person with **power to dispose** of any premises to **discriminate** against a disabled person:

- in the terms on which he or she offers to dispose of those premises to the disabled person; or

- by refusing to dispose of those premises to the disabled person; or

- in his or her treatment of the disabled person in relation to any list of persons in need of premises of that description.

These provisions are explained below. The disposal of premises includes selling or letting them.

s 22(3)   8.3   It is also unlawful for a person **managing** any premises to **discriminate** against a disabled person occupying those premises:

- in the way he or she permits the disabled person to make use of any benefits or facilities; or

- by refusing (or deliberately omitting) to permit the disabled person to make use of any benefits or facilities; or

- by evicting the disabled person or subjecting the disabled person to any other detriment.

These provisions are explained below.

8.4 It is also unlawful for a person whose **licence or consent** is required for the disposal of any leased or sub-let premises to **discriminate** against a disabled person by withholding that licence or consent.

s 22(4)

These provisions are explained below.

What does the Act mean by "discrimination"?

8.5 For the purposes of the provisions in relation to premises, a person discriminates against a disabled person if he or she:

s 24(1)

- **treats the disabled person less favourably**, for a reason relating to the disabled person's disability, than he or she treats (or would treat) others to whom that reason does not (or would not) apply; **and**

- cannot show that the treatment is **justified**.

The concept of less favourable treatment for a reason related to a disabled person's disability is discussed in **Chapter 3** above. Whether less favourable treatment of a disabled person in relation to premises is capable of being justified is discussed below.

A landlord asks a deaf person for a non-refundable deposit as a condition of him renting a flat. Other tenants are simply asked for a refundable deposit. This is less favourable treatment for a reason relating to his disability. Unless justified, this is likely to be unlawful.

The owner of an office block refuses to lease office space to a disabled self-employed businesswoman. This is because the owner has evidence that she is bankrupt and would be unable to pay the rent. The less favourable treatment of the disabled person is not for a reason related to her disability and is likely to be lawful.

A housing association has a blanket policy of requiring all new tenants with a history of mental health problems to have only a short term tenancy in the first instance. This is so that the association can see whether such tenants are suitable. This policy is not applied to other new tenants and is likely to be unlawful.

Is there a duty to make adjustments in relation to premises?

8.6 There is no legal duty to make reasonable adjustments to premises which are sold, let or managed. Although there is nothing in the Act to prohibit positive action in favour of disabled people, those who are selling, letting or managing premises do not have to make adjustments to make those premises more suitable for disabled people. However, persons managing or disposing of premises may also be service providers (for example, estate agencies, accommodation bureaux or management companies). In that respect they will have to ensure that the services which they provide are accessible to disabled people (see **Chapters 4 and 5** generally and the example in paragraph 5.33).

What is a "disposal" under the Act?

s 22(6)   8.7 The Act covers both the sale and lease of premises, and any other form of legal disposal (for example, by licence). It includes the grant of a right to occupy the premises. Where the premises are comprised in or the subject of a tenancy, they include:

- assigning (or the assignation of) the tenancy; or

- sub-letting the premises or any part of them; or

- parting with possession of the premises or any part of them.

Disposing of premises does not, however, include the hire of premises or the booking of rooms in hotels or guest houses. These are covered by the provisions relating to services (see **Chapters 2 – 6** above).

What is meant by "premises" and "tenancy"?

s 22(8)
s 68(1)   8.8 The Act only applies to premises in the United Kingdom. Premises include land of any description. For example, dwelling-houses, office blocks, flats, bed-sits, factory premises, industrial or commercial sites, and agricultural land are covered by these provisions.

s 22(6)   8.9 The Act applies to the granting and assignment of tenancies and sub-leases. A tenancy includes a tenancy created:

- by a lease or sub-lease; or

- by an agreement for a lease or sub-lease; or

- by a tenancy agreement; or

- by or under any enactment (for example, a statutory tenancy).

Does the Act apply to all disposals of premises?

8.10 The Act does not apply to every disposal of premises. The provisions which prohibit discrimination against disabled people by a person with a power to dispose of premises do not apply to an owner-occupier if:

s 22(2)

- that person owns an estate or interest in the premises; and

- wholly occupies the premises.

8.11 However, if the owner-occupier:

s 22(2)

- uses the services of an estate agent; or

s 22(a)

- publishes, or arranges to be published, an advertisement or notice (whether to the public or not),

s 22(b)

for the purpose of disposing of the premises, that is a disposal of premises to which the Act applies. An estate agent is anyone carrying on a trade or profession providing services for the purpose of finding premises for people seeking to acquire them or assisting in the disposal of premises. This includes letting agents.

s 22(6)

Disposal of premises

8.12 It is unlawful for a person with power to dispose of any premises to discriminate against a disabled person (see paragraphs 8.2 and 8.5 above). A person includes a legal entity such as a company.

s 22(1)

Terms of disposal

8.13 It is unlawful to discriminate in the terms on which a person with power to dispose of premises offers to dispose of those premises to a disabled person.

s 22(1)(a)

> A landlord charges a disabled tenant a higher rent for a flat than the landlord would have charged a non-disabled tenant. This is likely to be unlawful.

A house owner agrees to sell his house to a disabled person, subject to contract. He requires the disabled person to pay a 25 per cent deposit as a condition of continuing with the sale. The house owner would not ask for such a large deposit from a non-disabled person. This is likely to be unlawful.

As a condition of granting a tenancy to a disabled person with muscular dystrophy, a housing association insists that the disabled person signs an agreement that she will not apply for aids and adaptations during the tenancy. This is likely to be against the law.

Refusal of disposal

s 22(1)(b)   8.14 It is unlawful for a person with power to dispose of premises to discriminate by refusing to dispose of those premises to a disabled person.

A commercial landlord refuses to let office space to a self-employed businessman who had Hodgkin's disease five years ago but is now fully recovered. Without any supporting evidence, the landlord believes that his former disability may recur and that he will then be unable to keep up the rent payments. This is likely to be unlawful.

Treatment in relation to housing lists

s 22(1)(c)   8.15 It is unlawful for a person with power to dispose of any premises to discriminate against a disabled person in his or her treatment of that disabled person in relation to any list of people in need of such premises.

A private letting agency refuses to place people with any form of disability on its waiting lists. This is likely to be unlawful.

A person has been on a council housing list for some time. He is then involved in a serious motor accident resulting in permanent paraplegia (paralysis of the legs). Despite the fact that suitable housing is available for him, the council allocates housing to other people who have been on the list for a shorter period than the newly-disabled person, simply because of his disability. This is likely to be unlawful.

Exemption for small dwellings

8.16 The provisions of the Act prohibiting discrimination against disabled people in the disposal of premises do not apply to certain small dwellings. This exemption only applies to houses or other residential property. It does not apply to commercial or industrial premises. A number of conditions must be satisfied before a small dwelling is exempted. — s 23(1)

8.17 First, the person with the power to dispose of the premises (or whose licence or consent is required for the disposal), referred to in the Act as the **"relevant occupier"**, must:

- reside on the premises; and — s 23(2)(a)

- intend to continue to reside on the premises; and — s 23(2)(a)

- be sharing accommodation on the premises with other people who are not members of the relevant occupier's household. — s 23(2)(b)

    The "relevant occupier" includes a "near relative" of the person concerned. A "near relative" for this purpose means a person's spouse (i.e. husband or wife), partner, parent, child, grandparent, grandchild, or brother or sister (whether of full or half blood or through marriage). The term "partner" means the other member of a couple consisting of a man and a woman who are not married to each other but are living together as husband and wife. — s 23(6)–(7)

8.18 Second, the shared accommodation must not be storage accommodation or a means of access. — s 23(2)(c)

8.19 Third, the premises must be "small premises". — s 23(2)(d)

When are premises "small premises"?

8.20 Premises are "small premises" if the following conditions are satisfied: — s 23(3)–(4)

- only the "relevant occupier" and members of his or her household reside in the accommodation occupied by him or her; and — s 23(4)(a)

- the premises include residential accommodation for at least one other household; and — s 23(4)(b) s 23(4)c

- other residential accommodation is let (or is available for letting) on a separate tenancy or similar agreement for each other household; and

s 23(4)d

- there are not normally more than two such other households.

> The basement and ground floor of a large Victorian house have been converted into two self-contained flats which are let to tenants under separate tenancies by the house owner. The house owner and her family continue to reside exclusively in the remaining floors of the house. The house satisfies the Act's definition of small premises (but the house may still not be exempt from the Act, see paragraph 8.22 below).

s 23(3)
s 23(5)

8.21 Alternatively, premises are "small premises" if there is not normally residential accommodation on the premises for more than six people in addition to the "relevant occupier" and any members of his or her household.

> The owner of a four bedroomed detached house has converted two bedrooms into bed-sit accommodation for two people. He continues to live in the house with his family. The house satisfies the Act's definition of small premises.

When does the small dwellings exemption apply?

8.22 The small dwellings exemption is likely to apply to a multi-occupancy residential building with shared accommodation. All the conditions in paragraphs 8.17 to 8.20 or 8.21 above must be satisfied if the exemption is to apply.

> The converted Victorian house in the example in paragraph 8.20 above has a communal entrance door and hallway giving private access to the two flats and the remainder of the house. Although the house satisfies the definition of small premises, the small dwellings exemption does not apply. This is because the owner of the house resides on the premises but does not share any accommodation (other than means of access) with the tenants of the two self-contained flats.

The four bedroomed detached house in the example in paragraph 8.21 above has a bathroom and kitchen which is shared by the owner (and his family) with the tenants of the bed-sit rooms. Not only does the house satisfy the definition of small premises, it is also subject to the small dwellings exemption. This is because the house owner lives in the house and shares some accommodation (other than access or storage accommodation) with the tenants of the bed-sit rooms.

Management of premises

8.23 It is unlawful for a person managing any premises to discriminate against a disabled person occupying those premises (see paragraphs 8.3 and 8.5 above). A person includes a legal entity such as a company.

s 22(3)

Who is a "person managing any premises"?

8.24 The Act is not simply concerned with discrimination against disabled people by property owners in relation to premises. A property management agency, accommodation bureau, housekeeper, estate agent or rent collection service may also be liable under the Act for discrimination in connection with managing premises, as would the managing agents of commercial premises.

Use of benefits or facilities

8.25 It is unlawful for a person managing any premises to discriminate against a disabled person occupying those premises:

- in the way he or she permits the disabled person to make use of any benefits or facilities; or

  s 22(3)(a)

- by refusing or deliberately omitting to permit the disabled person to make use of any benefits or facilities.

  s 22(3)(b)

Benefits or facilities include, for example, laundry facilities, access to a garden and parking facilities.

A property management company manages and controls a residential block of flats on behalf of the landlord-owner. The block has a basement swimming pool and a communal garden for use by the tenants. A disabled tenant with a severe disfigurement is told by the company that he can only use the swimming pool at restricted times because other tenants feel uncomfortable in his presence. This is likely to be unlawful.

71

The company also refuses to allow the disabled child of one of the tenants to use the communal garden. The child has attention deficit disorder and other tenants object to his use of the garden. This is likely to be unlawful.

Eviction

s 22(3)(c)

8.26 It is unlawful for a person managing any premises to discriminate against a disabled person occupying those premises by evicting the disabled person. This prohibition does not prevent the eviction of a disabled tenant where the law allows it, for example, where he or she is in arrears of rent or has breached other terms of the tenancy, and where the reason for the eviction is not related to disability. However, in each case, appropriate court action needs to be taken to obtain an eviction order.

A tenant of a house has recently been diagnosed with AIDS. His landlord gives him a week's notice to quit the house, although he is not in arrears of rent or otherwise in breach of his tenancy. This is likely to be unlawful.

Other detriment

s 22(3)(c)

8.27 It is unlawful for a person managing any premises to discriminate against a disabled person occupying those premises by subjecting him or her to any other detriment. This includes subjecting disabled people to harassment (or failing to prevent them being subjected to harassment by others), for example, physical attack, damage to their property, verbal abuse and other similar behaviour, which deprives them of the peaceful enjoyment of their premises.

A block of flats is managed by a management committee of tenants. The members of the committee harass a disabled tenant who has sickle cell disease and who is mobility impaired. They believe that her use of a wheelchair causes above average wear and tear to the doors and carpets in communal areas, and that this will lead to an increase in their annual maintenance charges. This is likely to be unlawful.

Small dwellings exemption

8.28 The small dwellings exemption explained in paragraphs 8.16 – 8.22 above applies equally to alleged discrimination in the management of premises.

s 23(1)

Licence or consent

8.29 It is unlawful for any person whose licence or consent is required for the disposal of any premises, comprised in or the subject of a tenancy, to discriminate against a disabled person by withholding that licence or consent (see paragraphs 8.4 and 8.5 above). A person includes a legal entity such as a company. It is irrelevant whether the tenancy was created before or after the passing of the Act.

s 22(4)–(5)

> A tenant of a house occupies the premises under a tenancy agreement with a right to sub-let the house with the prior consent of the landlord-owner. The tenant is being posted to work abroad for a year. He wishes to sub-let the house to a disabled person who has partial paralysis as a result of polio. The owner of the house refuses to consent to the sub-letting. She wrongly assumes that the disabled person will be unable to keep up rent payments and may cause damage to the fabric of the house. This is likely to be unlawful.

Small dwellings exemption

8.30 The small dwellings exemption explained in paragraphs 8.16 – 8.22 above applies equally to alleged discrimination in relation to the withholding of a licence or consent.

s 23(1)
s 23(6)(b)

Justifying less favourable treatment in relation to premises

8.31 Less favourable treatment of a disabled person for a reason relating to disability amounts to discrimination unless that treatment can be shown to be justified.

s 24(1)(b)

8.32 Treating a disabled person less favourably for a reason related to disability may be justified **only if**:

s 24(2)

- he or she believes that one or more of the conditions in paragraph 8.33 below are satisfied; **and**

s 24(2)(a)

- it is reasonable in all the circumstances of the case for that person to hold that opinion.

s 24(2)(b)

8.33 The Act sets out four possible conditions which could apply, but for ease of explanation this Code sets them out under three headings:

- health or safety;

- incapacity to contract;

- treatment necessary in order for the disabled person or other occupiers to use a benefit or facility.

As will be seen, these conditions do not apply to all forms of discrimination in relation to premises.

8.34 At the time of the alleged discrimination, the person said to be discriminating must reasonably believe that one of those conditions is satisfied to justify less favourable treatment. These conditions are similar to (but not exactly the same as) the conditions that apply to justifying discrimination in the provision of services. The general approach to justification is the same (see paragraphs 6.7 to 6.9 above).

Health or safety

8.35 In any case of alleged discrimination in relation to the disposal or management of premises (or the withholding of a licence or consent), the less favourable treatment of a disabled person may be justified only if it is reasonably believed that the treatment is necessary in order not to endanger the health or safety of any person, including the disabled person in question.

> A landlord refuses to let a third floor flat to a disabled person who has had a stroke resulting in mobility problems and who lives alone. The disabled person is clearly unable to negotiate the stairs in safety or use the fire escape or other escape routes in an emergency. The landlord believes that there is a health or safety risk to the disabled person. Provided it is reasonable for the landlord to hold that opinion, the refusal to let is likely to be justified.

A landlord refuses to let a flat to someone with AIDS, believing him to be a health risk to other tenants. The prospective tenant provides the landlord with Government literature confirming that AIDS is not a health risk, but the landlord continues to refuse to let the flat. The landlord's opinion that the prospective tenant is a health risk is unlikely to be a reasonable one for the landlord to hold. The refusal to let is unlikely to be justified.

Incapacity to contract

8.36 In any case of alleged discrimination in relation to the disposal or management of premises (or the withholding of a licence or consent), the less favourable treatment of a disabled person may be justified if it is reasonably believed that the disabled person is incapable of entering into an enforceable agreement or of giving an informed consent, and for that reason the treatment is reasonable in the particular case.

s 24(3)(b)

The owner of a lock-up garage refuses to rent it to a person with a learning disability. Despite the owner attempting to explain that she expects to be paid a weekly rent for the garage, the disabled person appears incapable of understanding the legal obligation involved. The garage owner believes that the disabled person is incapable of entering into an enforceable agreement. This is likely to be a reasonable opinion for the garage owner to hold and the refusal to rent the garage is therefore likely to be justified.

However, if the disabled person in the above example offers to pay rent monthly in advance, or if his friend is able to act as guarantor for payment of the rent, the refusal to rent the garage is unlikely to be reasonable and would therefore not be justified.

Treatment necessary in order for the disabled person or other occupiers to use a benefit or facility

8.37 In a case of alleged discrimination by a person managing premises:

s 24(3)(c)–(d)

- in the way a disabled person occupying the premises is permitted to make use of any benefit or facility; or

- by refusing (or deliberately omitting) to permit a disabled person occupying the premises to make use of any benefit or facility,

less favourable treatment of the disabled person may be justified if it is reasonably believed that the treatment is necessary for the disabled person or occupiers of other premises forming part of the building to make use of the benefit or facility.

> A disabled tenant with a mobility impairment is prevented by the management agency of a block of flats from parking in front of the main entrance to the block. The agency requires him to park in the car park at the back of the block. Although this causes the disabled tenant inconvenience and difficulty, the reason for the agency's decision is that there is insufficient space at the front of the building and the disabled tenant's car frequently causes an obstruction to other tenants. The decision is likely to be justified.

> A landlord refuses to allow a disabled tenant with a learning disability to use the shared laundry facilities in a block of flats because the disabled tenant frequently breaks the washing machines. She does not understand the instructions. The landlord's refusal is likely to be justified.

Deposits

SI 1996/1836

8.38 A person with power to dispose of any premises may be prepared to grant a tenant a right to occupy the premises on the condition that the tenant pays a deposit. The deposit is usually refundable at the end of the occupation if the premises and its contents are undamaged. The Regulations provide special rules to deal with the question of whether the person with power to dispose of the premises can refuse to return the disabled tenant's deposit in full.

reg 7(1)

8.39 The special rules apply where, in relation to a deposit, a person with power to dispose of the premises:

- for a reason which relates to a disabled person's disability

- treats a disabled person less favourably

- than it treats (or would treat) others to whom that reason does not (or would not) apply.

8.40 Less favourable treatment of a disabled person in respect of a deposit may be justified if **all** the following conditions are satisfied:

reg 7(2)

- the person with power to dispose of the premises has granted the disabled person a right to occupy premises (whether under a formal tenancy agreement or otherwise);

- the disabled person is required to provide a deposit;

- the deposit is refundable at the end of the occupation if the premises and its contents are undamaged;

- damage has occurred to the premises or its contents for a reason which relates to the disabled person's disability;

- the person with the power to dispose of the premises refuses to refund some or all of the deposit;

- that refusal is because the damage is above the level at which he or she would normally refund the deposit in full;

- the refusal is reasonable in all the circumstances of the case.

> A disabled person rents a flat for 12 months. The landlord requires all tenants to pay a deposit against damage to the flat and its furnishings. Because of the nature of her disability, the disabled person uses a wheelchair. In this particular case, it causes abnormal wear and tear to the carpets and floorings in the flat. At the end of the tenancy, the landlord retains part of the deposit against the cost of repairing the damage. This is likely to be justified.

8.41 The special rules on deposits do not justify a person with power to dispose of premises charging a disabled person a higher deposit than it would charge to other people. Similarly, a person with power to dispose of premises is not justified in charging a disabled person a deposit where he or she would not expect other people to pay such a deposit. In either case, this could amount to unlawful discrimination in the terms on which the premises are offered for disposal to the disabled person.

s 22(1)(a)

reg 7(2)   8.42 Where a person with power to dispose of premises requires a disabled person to pay a deposit, he or she may only refuse to repay the deposit if any damage to the premises or its contents is above the level at which he or she would normally refund the deposit in full. If the damage is of a level where he or she would normally repay the deposit in full, a disabled person must not be treated less favourably than any other person who has paid a deposit and has caused comparable damage to the premises or its contents.

reg 7(2)   8.43 A refusal to refund a deposit to a disabled person must be reasonable in all the circumstances of the case. A person with power to dispose of premises is unlikely to be justified in withholding the whole or part of a deposit if the amount withheld exceeds the loss suffered by that person as a result of the damage.

Other provisions under the Act

Introduction

9.1 A number of other provisions of the Act are relevant to understanding the protection which the Act affords disabled people in respect of services and premises. These provisions also assist service providers (and those selling, letting or managing premises) to appreciate the extent of their responsibilities under the legislation.

Victimisation

9.2 Victimisation is a special form of discrimination covered by the Act. It applies whether or not the person victimised is a disabled person. For the purposes of Part III of the Act, victimisation is treated as discrimination. Victimisation is unlawful if it occurs in relation to the provision of services or in relation to the selling, letting or management of premises.

s 55
s 19(4)
s 22
s 19
s 22

9.3 The Act also says that a person discriminates against another person (the victim) if he or she treats the victim less favourably than he or she treats (or would treat) other people in the same circumstances, – disregarding the victim's disability – because the victim has:

s 55(1)
s 55(2)(a)
s 55(3)

- brought proceedings under the Act (whether or not proceedings are later withdrawn); **or**

- given evidence or information in connection with such proceedings; **or**

- done anything else under the Act; **or**

- alleged someone has contravened the Act (whether or not the allegation is later dropped).

A non-disabled person acts as a witness in a complaint by a disabled person of disability discrimination by a police officer. Later, in retaliation, other police officers refuse to provide to the non-disabled person local crime prevention services which the police provide to the public. This is victimisation and is likely to be unlawful.

9.4 The Act also says that a person discriminates against another person (the victim) if he or she treats the victim less favourably than he or she treats (or would treat) other people in the same circumstances – disregarding the victim's disability – because he or she believes or suspects that the victim had done or intends to do any of the above things.

9.5 However, it is not victimisation to treat a person less favourably because that person has made an allegation which was false and not made in good faith.

> A disabled person makes an allegation in a local newspaper that a local pub discriminates against disabled people. That allegation is untrue and is made without any foundation as part of a personal vendetta against the publican. The publican subsequently bars the disabled person from the pub. In the circumstances, this is not victimisation and is unlikely to be unlawful.

Aiding unlawful acts

9.6 The Act says that a person who knowingly helps someone else to do something made unlawful by the Act is also to be treated as having done the same kind of unlawful act.

> A bartender refuses to serve a party of disabled customers. Although the manager of the bar knows this is against the law, she takes no action to reprimand the bartender and refuses to discuss the matter when the disabled customers complain to her. It is likely that the bartender is acting unlawfully and the manager might also be liable for aiding him.

9.7 A person does not knowingly aid someone else to do something unlawful if:

- that other person makes a statement to him or her that it would not be unlawful because of any provision of the Act; **and**

- he or she acts in reliance on that statement; **and**

- it is reasonable to rely on the statement.

A person who knowingly or recklessly makes such a statement which is false or misleading in a material respect is guilty of a criminal offence and will be liable on conviction to a fine up to level 5 on the standard scale (£5,000 as of May 1996).

> The owner of a small newsagent's shop tells his staff that the provisions of the Act on providing services do not apply to small businesses. The owner knows this is not legally correct. He instructs his staff to refuse to serve disabled customers who are patients at a psychiatric clinic next door. Relying on the owner's statement, the staff follow those instructions. It is likely that the shop owner is acting unlawfully and has committed a criminal offence, but it is unlikely that the staff are liable for knowingly aiding an unlawful act.

Liability for employees' and agents' acts

9.8 The Act says that employers are responsible for anything done by their employees in the course of their employment. A service provider (and a person selling, letting or managing premises) may be an employer. It is not a defence for the employer simply to show that the act took place without its knowledge or approval. If the employer is liable for the act of an employee in this way, the employee might also be treated as having knowingly aided the employer to do the act (see paragraphs 9.6 and 9.7 above).

s 58(1)

s 57(2)

> A waiter in a café refuses to serve a disabled customer whom he knows has had tuberculosis in the past. He wrongly believes that the customer still has an infectious disease. It is likely that the refusal of service is unlawful. Although the owner of the café is unaware that this is happening, the owner may be liable under the Act. The waiter might also be liable if he has knowingly aided the employer.

9.9 If a claim under the Act is made against an employer based on anything done by an employee, it is a defence that the employer took such steps as were reasonably practicable to prevent such acts. It is important that employers should develop policies on disability matters and communicate these

s 58(5)

to their employees. All staff should be made aware that it is unlawful to discriminate against disabled people. Further guidance is provided in **Chapter 10** below.

> Unknown to her employer, the receptionist in an estate agent refuses to give details of houses for rent to a client with a mental health condition. The estate agent has issued clear instructions to its staff about their obligations under the Act, has provided disability awareness training, and regularly checks that staff are complying with the law. It is likely that the receptionist has acted unlawfully but that her employer will have a defence under the Act.

s 58(2)–(3)

s 57(2)

9.10 Service providers (and those selling, letting or managing premises) are also liable for anything done by their agents, if done with their authority. That authority may be express or implied and may have been given before or after the act in question. The agent may also be taken to have aided the service provider (or those selling, letting or managing premises) to have committed an unlawful act.

Terms of agreements

s 26(1)

9.11 Any term in an agreement is void (that is, unenforceable) if its effect is to:

- require someone to do something which would be unlawful under Part III of the Act (the part relating to services and premises);

- exclude or limit the operation of Part III; or

- prevent someone making a claim under Part III.

s 26(2)

However, an agreement to settle or compromise a claim brought under the Act is not affected by this rule.

> A landlord's lease includes a term allowing a tenant to sub-let the premises, but the term forbids the tenant from sub-letting to people with learning disabilities. This term is not legally binding.

A travel agent accepts a booking from a disabled customer for a holiday at an hotel in the UK. The terms of booking exclude any liability of the travel agent or the hotel under the Act. This term is not legally binding.

Statutory authority and national security

9.12 A service provider (or person selling, letting or managing premises) is not required to do anything under the Act that will result in a breach of legal obligations under any other legislation or enactment. Nothing in the Act makes unlawful anything done for the purpose of safeguarding national security.

s 59

What happens if there is a dispute under the Act?

9.13 A person who believes that a service provider (or person selling, letting or managing premises) has unlawfully discriminated against him or her may bring civil proceedings. Those proceedings take place in the county court in England and Wales (in Scotland, the sheriff court) or, in respect of insurance services provided to employees, the employment tribunals. Similar proceedings may also be brought against a person who has aided someone else to commit an unlawful act. Court action must be brought within six months of the alleged discrimination (the time limit is three months in the employment tribunal).

s 25(1)
s 25(3)–(4)
Sch 3 para 6

9.14 Before legal proceedings are begun, it may be sensible to raise a complaint with the service provider (or person selling, letting or managing premises) to see whether the issue can be determined to the satisfaction of both parties. Even when legal proceedings have been brought, the service provider (or person selling, letting, or managing premises) may wish to attempt to settle the matter through discussion with the complainant. Any discrimination may have been unintentional and the dispute may be capable of being resolved by negotiation.

9.15 The Disability Access Rights Advice Service (DARAS) has been established under the Act. DARAS provides free advice to national and local agencies advising disabled people and businesses on the application of Part III of the Act. DARAS cannot give advice directly to members of the public.

s 28

9.16 Where DARAS has been approached for advice within six months of an alleged act of discrimination, the time limit for bringing an action in the courts is extended by two months.

9.17 There is also an independent conciliation service accessible via DARAS, operated by the ADR Group, which offers assistance to the public and service providers with a view to promoting the settlement of disputes under Part III of the Act without recourse to the courts.

What happens if a dispute cannot be resolved?

9.18 If a dispute cannot be resolved by conciliation or agreement, and the complainant has brought legal proceedings, the matter will have to be decided by a court. If successful, a disabled person could be awarded compensation for any financial loss, including injury to feelings. The disabled person may also seek an injunction (in Scotland, an interdict) to prevent the service provider (or person selling, letting or managing premises) repeating any discriminatory act in the future. The court may make a declaration as to the rights and responsibilities of the parties involved.

Disability Rights Commission

9.19 The Government is taking steps to establish a Disability Rights Commission from 2000. The Commission will have powers to work towards the elimination of discrimination and promote the equalisation of opportunity in respect of the provision of services to disabled people. In particular, the proposed Commission will be enabled to keep the Act under review, supply assistance and support to disabled litigants under the Act, provide information and advice to anyone with rights or obligations under the Act, carry out formal investigations, prepare new or revised Codes of Practice, and arrange independent conciliation of disputes under the legislation.

General guidance on good practice

Introduction

10.1 The Act requires service providers to plan ahead to meet the requirements of their disabled customers. Where necessary and reasonable, service providers should adjust the way they provide their services so that disabled people can use them. There are estimated to be around 8.6 million disabled people in Great Britain and they have considerable collective spending power. Adjustments for disabled people may also benefit other customers (and staff), enabling service providers to improve their overall level of service and gain more customers.

10.2 Discrimination is often unintentional or unwitting and may stem from a lack of awareness about disability. It may also result from mistaken assumptions or decisions based on speculation, generalisations or stereotypes. A service provider might wrongly assume that it could not cope with serving a disabled person or that a particular service would be of no interest or benefit to a disabled person. Where there is any doubt, service providers should ask disabled people – whether disabled customers or employees, or local or national disability organisations – how best they can be served. In particular, disability organisations have wide-ranging knowledge of the requirements of disabled people. Assistance might be obtained by contacting the DDA Helpline (see paragraph 1.13 above).

10.3 Service providers need to think about their attitude towards disabled people and the way they and their staff treat customers (**see Chapter 3**). Service providers are more likely to be able to comply with their duties under the Act if they:

- inform all staff dealing with the public that it is unlawful to discriminate against disabled people;

- establish a positive policy on the provision of services to ensure inclusion of disabled people and communicate it to all staff;

- train staff to understand the service provider's policy towards disabled people, their legal obligations and the duty of reasonable adjustments;

- monitor the implementation and effectiveness of such a policy;

- provide disability awareness and disability etiquette training for all staff who have contact with the public;

- address acts of disability discrimination by staff as part of disciplinary rules and procedures;

- have a customer complaints procedure which is easy for disabled people to use;

- consult with disabled customers, disabled staff and disability organisations;

- regularly review whether their services are accessible to disabled people.

How far it is reasonable for a service provider to undertake these actions depends on its size and resources and its particular circumstances.

10.4   In all cases, it is important to ensure that the dignity of a disabled person is respected when services are provided. Discrimination against disabled people often involves treatment which would be regarded as humiliating if accorded to other people. Making separate or segregated provision for disabled people might amount to less favourable treatment rather than equal opportunity. Disabled people are entitled to be consulted about how they might be served. Unfounded assumptions about what is best for them should not be made or acted upon. Disabled people are entitled to make the same choices and to take the same risks within the same limits as other people.

Good practice and reasonable adjustments

10.5   Service providers also have a duty to make reasonable adjustments for disabled people to enable them to access services (see **Chapters 4 and 5**). They may be initially unaware that any disabled people have had difficulty in accessing their services. Service providers should not assume that this means that they do not need to make adjustments. Reviewing the way services are provided helps service providers to check whether disabled people are being deterred by any physical or non-physical barriers. Making adjustments to overcome such barriers enables disabled people to access the services and could open up an entirely new customer base.

10.6 Service providers are more likely to be able to comply with their duty to make reasonable adjustments under the Act if they:

- audit physical and non-physical barriers to access for disabled people;

- make adjustments and put them in place;

- provide training to staff which is relevant to the adjustments to be made;

- draw the adjustments to the attention of disabled people;

- let disabled people know how to request assistance; and

- regularly review the effectiveness of adjustments and act on the findings of that review.

How far it is reasonable for a service provider to undertake these actions depends on its size and resources and its particular circumstances.

10.7 It is important that service providers do not assume that the only way to make services more accessible to disabled people would be to make a physical alteration to their premises (such as installing a permanent ramp or widening a doorway) which the Act does not require at present. Often, minor measures, such as allowing more time to deal with a disabled customer, help disabled people to use a service. In many cases, action such as disability awareness training is appropriate. Although physical alterations will not be required until 2004, such adjustments may be the only answer if other adjustments are not sufficient to overcome barriers to access. Service providers may wish to consider making such physical alterations now as part of a positive policy towards making their services accessible.

10.8 The best solution is often the simplest and most practicable. Listening carefully and responding to what disabled people really want helps service providers find the best way of meeting disabled people's requirements and expectations. However, this does not mean that in every case a service provider only has to take minor steps towards making its services accessible. The law may require service providers to give further thought and to take further action.

10.9 A service provider knows its business best and should be able to identify the more obvious physical or other barriers or impediments to access by disabled people to its services. It is good practice for a service provider to review the way it delivers its services to the public to discover whether there are any less obvious or unintentional problems of access for disabled people. A service provider might carry out periodic disability audits of its premises and business.

10.10 As a matter of good practice, a service provider should seek the views of disabled customers and disabled staff. Disabled people know best what hurdles they face in trying to use the services provided. They can help identify difficulties in accessing services and might also suggest solutions involving the provision of reasonable adjustments. Local and national disability groups or organisations of disabled people have extensive experience which service providers can draw on.

10.11 It might not be possible to anticipate every difficulty which a disabled person might have in accessing or using services. When considering the provision of a reasonable adjustment, a service provider should be flexible in its approach. It should try to anticipate the types of problems which could arise and should make every effort to know who its customers are.

10.12 If a service provider adopts good practice, it is unlikely that the law will be broken if it is not reasonable for the service provider to anticipate:

- a particular barrier or other impediment; or

- the requirements of people with particular disabilities; or

- the benefit of providing a particular reasonable adjustment.

10.13 However, once a service provider has become aware of the requirements of a particular disabled person who uses or seeks to use its services, it might then become reasonable for the service provider to take a particular step. This is especially so where a disabled person has pointed out the difficulty which he or she faces in accessing services, or has suggested a reasonable solution to that difficulty. It might be reasonable to take a particular temporary step immediately, even if this is not the best long term solution.

10.14 Once a service provider has decided to put a reasonable adjustment in place, it is important to draw its existence to the attention of disabled people. The service provider should also establish a means for letting the disabled person know how to request assistance. This ensures that the service provider is not only complying with the Act but is also adopting good practice. It encourages disabled people to regard its services as accessible. This might be done by a simple sign or notice at the entrance to the service provider's premises or at a service point. Alternatively, the availability of a reasonable adjustment might be highlighted in forms or documents used by the service provider, such as publicity materials. In all cases, it is important to use a means of communication which is itself accessible to disabled people.

> A city centre department store has a qualified British Sign Language interpreter who is a member of its sales staff. The store publicises this fact by using the international symbol at the entrance to the store and at the sales points.

> A supermarket is willing to provide an assisted shopping service to disabled customers. A suitably worded notice at the entrance to the supermarket and a regular public address announcement draws attention to this auxiliary service.

> An airport provides transfer by electric buggy between terminals and gates for passengers with a mobility disability. Prominent signs at the entrance to the arrivals and departures halls and at check-in desks allow disabled passengers to access that auxiliary service.

> A hospital has its forms and explanatory literature in accessible alternative formats such as large print, audio tape and Braille. A prominent note to that effect on the literature sent to patients, or a specific mention of this by reception staff when a patient first visits the hospital, assists disabled patients to access the service.

10.15 Staff training is also an important factor in providing reasonable adjustments. Staff should be generally aware of the requirements of disabled people and should appreciate how to respond appropriately to requests for a reasonable adjustment. They should know how to provide an auxiliary service and how to use any auxiliary aids which the service provider has. Staff should be encouraged to acquire additional skills in dealing with disabled people, for example, communicating with hearing impaired people and those with speech impairments.

10.16 Once a service provider has decided to make a reasonable adjustment, it is important to keep it under review. What was originally a reasonable step to take might no longer be sufficient and the provision of further or different adjustments might have to be considered. Equally, a step which might previously have been an unreasonable one for a service provider to have to take could subsequently become a reasonable step in the light of changed circumstances.

10.17 A service provider might wish to put in place positive practices which encourage disabled people to access its services. The effect of such an approach might also lead to the services being more accessible to its customers in general.

10.18 Service providers may also wish to anticipate the remaining duties in relation to physical features coming into force in 2004 (including providing an auxiliary aid which involves an alteration to the physical fabric of the building). Whenever a service provider is planning and executing building or refurbishment works, such as extending existing premises or making structural alterations to an existing building, it is sensible to provide for the removal or alteration of physical features which create a barrier to access for disabled people or to consider providing a reasonable means of avoiding the physical feature, even though the law does not yet require this. It might be more cost effective to make these alterations before 2004 and the Act does not prevent service providers from doing so.

A public launderette is installing new washing machines and tumble dryers. In doing so, the owners choose the machines and their positioning so as to facilitate their use by disabled customers. Although not yet required by law to do this, it has the effect of improving the accessibility of the launderette to disabled people.

A firm of accountants is refurbishing its offices. In replacing the carpets, the firm ensures that low pile, high density carpeting is fitted. This helps many of its clients with mobility disabilities (for example, those who use a wheelchair, artificial limb or walking aid) to move with greater ease within the office. The firm also decides to make improvements to the office lighting and signage. This aids its clients with visual or learning disabilities. As part of the refurbishment, the firm also fits Braille markings to lift buttons and installs a permanent induction loop system in one of its meeting rooms. The law does not require the firm to take these steps at present. By anticipating what the law will expect in future, the firm has placed itself in a good position to provide accessible services to its disabled clients.

Appendix:
The meaning of disability

This appendix is included to aid understanding about who is covered by the Act and should provide sufficient information on the definition of disability to cover the large majority of cases. The definition of disability in the Act is designed to cover only people who would generally be considered to be disabled. A Government publication, *Guidance on matters to be taken into account in determining questions relating to the definition of disability*, is also available.

When is a person disabled?
A person has a disability if he has a physical or mental impairment which has a substantial and long-term adverse effect on his ability to carry out normal day-to-day activities.

What about people who have recovered from a disability?
People who have had a disability within the definition are protected from discrimination even if they have since recovered.

What does "impairment" cover?
It covers physical or mental impairments; this includes sensory impairments, such as those affecting sight or hearing.

Are all mental impairments covered?
The term "mental impairment" is intended to cover a wide range of impairments relating to mental functioning, including what are often known as learning disabilities. However, the Act states that it does not include any impairment resulting from or consisting of a mental illness, unless that illness is a clinically well-recognised illness. A clinically well-recognised illness is one that is recognised by a respected body of medical opinion.

What is a "substantial" adverse effect?
A substantial adverse effect is something which is more than a minor or trivial effect. The requirement that an effect must be substantial reflects the general understanding of disability as a limitation going beyond the normal differences in ability which might exist among people.

What is a "long-term" effect?

A long-term effect of an impairment is one:

- which has lasted at least 12 months; or

- where the total period for which it lasts is likely to be at least 12 months; or

- which is likely to last for the rest of the life of the person affected.

Effects which are not long-term would therefore include loss of mobility due to a broken limb which is likely to heal within 12 months and the effects of temporary infections, from which a person would be likely to recover within 12 months.

What if the effects come and go over a period of time?

If an impairment has had a substantial adverse effect on normal day-to-day activities but that effect ceases, the substantial effect is treated as continuing if it is likely to recur; that is, if it is more probable than not that the effect will **recur**. Take the example of a person with rheumatoid arthritis whose impairment has a substantial adverse effect, which then ceases to be substantial (i.e. the person has a period of remission). The effects are to be treated as if they are continuing, and are likely to continue beyond 12 months, if:

- the impairment remains; and

- at least one recurrence of the substantial effect is likely to take place 12 months or more after the initial occurrence.

This would then be a long-term effect.

What are "normal day-to-day activities"?

They are activities which are carried out by most people on a fairly regular and frequent basis. The term is not intended to include activities which are normal only for a particular person or group of people, such as playing a musical instrument, or a sport, to a professional standard or performing a skilled or specialist task at work. However, someone who is affected in such a specialised way but is **also** affected in normal day-to-day activities would be covered by this part of the definition. The test of whether an impairment affects normal day-to-day activities is whether it affects one of the broad categories of capacity listed in Schedule 1 to the Act. They are:

- mobility;

- manual dexterity;

- physical co-ordination;

- continence;

- ability to lift, carry or otherwise move everyday objects;

- speech, hearing or eyesight;

- memory or ability to concentrate, learn or understand; or

- perception of the risk of physical danger.

What about treatment?
Someone with an impairment may be receiving medical or other treatment which alleviates or removes the effects (though not the impairment). In such cases, the treatment is ignored and the impairment is taken to have the effect it would have had without such treatment. This does not apply if substantial adverse effects are not likely to recur even if the treatment stops (i.e. the impairment has been cured).

Does this include people who wear spectacles?
No. The sole exception to the rule about ignoring the effects of treatment is the wearing of spectacles or contact lenses. In this case, the effect while the person is wearing spectacles or contact lenses should be considered.

Are people who have disfigurements covered?
People with severe disfigurements are covered by the Act. They do not need to demonstrate that the impairment has a substantial adverse effect on their ability to carry out normal day-to-day activities.

What about people who know their condition is going to get worse over time?
Progressive conditions are conditions which are likely to change and develop over time. Examples given in the Act are cancer, multiple sclerosis, muscular dystrophy and HIV infection. Where a person has a progressive condition he will be covered by the Act from the moment the condition leads to an impairment which has **some** effect on ability to carry out normal day-to-day activities, even though not a **substantial effect**, if that impairment is likely eventually to have a substantial adverse effect on such ability.

What about people who are registered disabled?

Those registered as disabled under the Disabled Persons (Employment) Act 1944 both on 12 January 1995 and 2 December 1996 will be treated as being disabled under the Disability Discrimination Act 1995 for three years from the latter date. At all times from 2 December 1996 onwards they will be covered by the Act as people who have had a disability. This does not preclude them from being covered as having a current disability any time after the three year period has finished. Whether they are or not will depend on whether they, like anyone else, meet the definition of disability in the Act.

Are people with genetic conditions covered?

If a genetic condition has no effect on ability to carry out normal day-to-day activities, the person is not covered. Diagnosis does not in itself bring someone within the definition. If the condition is progressive, then the rule about progressive conditions applies.

Are any conditions specifically excluded from the coverage of the Act?

Yes. Certain conditions are to be regarded as not amounting to impairments for the purposes of the Act. These are:

- addiction to or dependency on alcohol, nicotine, or any other substance (other than as a result of the substance being medically prescribed);

- seasonal allergic rhinitis (e.g. hayfever), except where it aggravates the effect of another condition;

- tendency to set fires;

- tendency to steal;

- tendency to physical or sexual abuse of other persons;

- exhibitionism;

- voyeurism.

Also disfigurements which consist of a tattoo (which has not been removed), non-medical body piercing, or something attached through such piercing, are to be treated as not having a substantial adverse effect on the person's ability to carry out normal day-to-day activities.

Index

Note: this index does not include the examples in boxes. References are to paragraph numbers.

accommodation – see *premises*
agents' acts, liability for 9.8
agreements, unenforceable terms of 9.11
aiding unlawful acts 9.6
alterations to premises – see *premises*
Alternative Disputes Resolution Group (ADR Group) 9.17
attorney, power of – see *power of attorney*
audiodescription 5.31
audio tape 5.16, 5.31
audio-visual
      fire alarms 5.28
      telephones 5.28
audits of premises – see *premises*
auxiliary aids or services 4.5, 5.14–5.35, 10.15, 10.18

blindness – see *visual impairments*
Braille 5.31, 5.35
British Sign Language 5.24
      – see also *sign language*
buildings, alterations to – see *premises*

charging 6.23–6.24, 7.17
Code of Practice
      purpose of 1.2
      status of 1.4, 1.7
colleges 2.19–2.20
colour coding 5.33
compensation 9.18
consent 8.29–8.30, 8.35
consultation 10.2–10.4, 10.8, 10.10
cost of adjustments 6.23–6.24
customer complaints procedures 10.3

damage to premises – see *premises*
DARAS – see *Disability Access Rights Advisory Service*
dates of coming into force *inside front cover*
deafblindness 5.27, 5.35
deafness – see *hearing disability*
deposits 6.3, 7.14–7.19
      justification for less favourable treatment 7.15–7.19

premises – see *premises*

designers 2.25–2.26

disabled person, definition of 2.9–2.11, *appendix*

Disability Access Rights Advice Service (DARAS) 9.15–9.17

Disability Discrimination Act 1995

    scope 1.1, 2.12–2.26

Disability Discrimination (Services and Premises) Regulations

    1996 6.15, 7.2

    1999 5.12, 5.19

Disability Rights Commission 9.19

discrimination

    by service providers 2.2–2.3, 2.5–2.8, 3.2–3.3

    definition of 2.4–2.8, 8.5

disposal of premises, definition of – see *premises*

disputes 9.13–9.18

education 2.18–2.19

employees' acts 9.8

eviction 8.26

exemptions 2.17–2.26

failure to comply 4.18, 6.5

fire regulations 6.11

guarantees 6.3, 7.9–7.13

guiding 5.31, 5.35

hearing disability 5.24, 5.27–5.28, 5.30, 5.35

housing lists 8.15

incapacity to contract – see *less favourable treatment,*
    justification for

induction loop systems 5.28, 5.35

inductive couplers 5.28

injunctions 9.18

insurance 6.3, 7.2–7.8

Internet 5.28

interpretation 5.16, 5.24, 5.28–5.29

justification for less favourable treatment – see *less favourable*
    treatment, justification for

landlords – see *premises*

large-print documents 5.31, 5.33

learning disabilities 5.27, 5.33

less favourable treatment 3.3–3.11

less favourable treatment, justification for 6.2, 6.4, 6.6–6.26

    deposits 7.15–7.19, 8.39

    enable provision of service 6.20

    greater expense 6.23

    guarantees 7.9–7.13

health or safety 6.10–6.12, 8.33, 8.35
incapacity to contract 6.13–6.16, 8.33, 8.36
insurance 7.3–7.8
otherwise unable to provide service 6.17
premises 8.5, 8.31
protecting nature of business or service 6.25
letting premises – see *premises*
licence 8.29–8.30, 8.35
lipreading 5.24
lipspeakers 5.28

managing premises – see *premises*
manufacturers 2.25–2.26
mental impairment 2.9–2.10
Moon 5.31, 5.35
more favourable treatment 3.18

National Disability Council 1.2
national security 9.12

permanent alterations 5.20
        – see also *premises*
physical features 4.6, 5.9–5.10, 5.19
        definition of 5.12
planning adjustments 10.1, 10.18
policies 10.3
        duty to change 4.4, 5.2–5.8
power of attorney 6.15
practice
        duty to change 4.4, 5.2–5.8
premises
        alterations to 4.6, 5.9–5.12, 10.7, 10.18
        audits of 10.6, 10.9
        damage to 8.27, 8.40, 8.42–8.43
        definition of 8.8
        deposits 8.38–8.43
        disposal of 8.10–8.22
        disposal of, definition 8.7
        letting 8.6, 8.11, 9.2
        managing 8.3, 8.6, 8.23–8.28, 9.2
        selling 8.6, 9.2
        shared 2.16, 8.17–8.19, 8.22
        small, exemptions for 8.16–8.22, 8.28, 8.30
private clubs 2.23–2.24
        definition of 2.24
procedures 10.3
        duty to change 4.4, 5.2–5.8

readers 5.31

reasonable adjustments 4.1–4.18, 5.7, 5.9–5.10, 6.16, 6.19, 6.22, 6.25–6.26, 8.6, 10.5–10.18
    auxiliary aids 4.14
    definition of 4.4–4.5
    failure to make 2.3, 4.2, 6.2, 6.5, 6.9, 6.12

reasonable steps 4.10–4.15, 5.3, 5.5–5.8, 5.13–5.14, 5.15, 5.22, 10.16

refusing service – see *service*

relevant occupier 8.17

schools 2.19–2.20

selling premises – see *premises*

service
    refusing 3.2, 3.12–3.14
    standards of 3.2, 3.15–3.16
    terms of 3.17

shared accommodation or premises – see *premises*

sign language 5.16, 5.28–5.29
    – see also *British Sign Language*

small premises, exemptions for – see *premises*

speech disability 5.27

standards of service – see *service*

statutory authority 9.12

subtitles 5.28

telephone amplifiers 5.28

telephone helplines 10.2

teletext 5.28

tenancy, definition of 8.9

terms of service – see *service*

textphones 5.28

touch facilities 5.31

training 10.3, 10.6, 10.15

transcription service 5.28

transport 2.18, 2.21–2.22

unenforceable terms of agreements – see *agreements*

unreasonably difficult 4.16–4.17, 5.2, 5.6

victimisation 9.2

videos 5.28

visual impairments 5.27, 5.31, 5.35

Printed in the United Kingdom for The Stationery Office.
J0083747, C60, 6/99, 5673.